God's Woman Revisited

GARY T. BURKE

GOD'S woman

REVISITED

POCKET EDITION

LUMINARE PRESS
WWW.LUMINAREPRESS.COM

Printed in the United States of America

Cover Design by Disciple Design

Luminare Press
442 Charnelton St.
Eugene, OR 97401
www.luminarepress.com

LCCN: 2020906828
ISBN: 978-1-64388-348-9

*This book is dedicated to God's women
and God's men as they seek to understand
and apply His will for their roles in the home,
in the church, and in the world at large.*

TABLE OF CONTENTS

CHAPTER ONE
God's Woman

CHAPTER TWO
The Current Impasse

CHAPTER THREE
What Disciplined Bible Study Looks Like

Preface

This book is an abridged version of the 2019 book, *God's Woman Revisited: Women and the Church*. While the original book has been well received, some have expressed a preference for an edition that is less technical and more manageable in length. *God's Woman Revisited: Pocket Edition* has been written with these readers in mind.

The abridged version mirrors the themes, chapter by chapter, of the original book. The author has attempted to include enough information from the earlier book to give adequate support for his conclusions without overburdening the reader with extra details. With these shorter chapters and discussion questions at the end of each of them, this book is well suited for both personal use and congregational Bible classes.

Readers will probably find some chapters more relevant to your interests than others and may want to approach the chapters out of order. They have been written on discrete enough topics that this can be done profitably. However, since certain themes are mentioned frequently and developed throughout the book, you will miss some of this continuity if you only read selectively. There is a deliberate flow in the book that will be lost if you do not read it from start to finish.

Foreword

Throughout Christian history, churches have felt the need to deal with issues that either threatened them personally (persecution), challenged fundamental biblical doctrines, or simply troubled the church. A century ago, several churches in the USA debated about which is the right church. A half century or so ago baptism was once again a discussed issue. Two or three decades ago, many articles and books were written on biblical interpretation, specifically focused on what was called the "new hermeneutic." For a couple of decades now, "women's place in the church" has claimed a deserved attention. Regardless of the causes of this interest, it is a biblical subject and causes difficulties in many churches.

Current approaches range from those who simply accommodate their church's practices to the prevailing cultural values, while at the other extreme some churches are so far right, through less-than-responsible handling of Scripture, that they end up stricter than God Himself! Gary Burke's approach is based on deep respect for Scripture and a keen interest in life in the local church. This is not the first time women's place in the church has been a point of concern and discussion among churches of Christ. As you will see, Burke stands on the shoulders of a formidable preacher who flourished over eighty years ago. Burke brings to the subject, however, a high level of exegesis that is clearly stated and carefully followed.

This Pocket Edition is appropriate. Many subjects are treated at different levels for readers who are in different positions in their understanding. In the 19th century, it was common for the British to write missionary biographies at two levels, one for children (planting seeds) and one for older readers who would appreciate greater details. Each was valuable in its own right. Similarly, this Pocket Edition of Burke's larger study by the same name preserves the essential line of thought, so that one can get at the subject more easily and quickly than would be the case of working through 350 pages. The text is sixty percent shorter than the larger volume. When one wonders how the author reached this or that conclusion, he or she can have access to technical matters in the larger book.

Like several other biblical subjects, the teachings about women in Scripture involve uncertainties at various points, and Burke identifies them. He is quick to state at times that "we just do not know." One's first task, however, is to ascertain what is *clearly* taught on any subject. To contribute to that, the author deals with the whole range of teachings about women, from the creation narratives in Genesis to the New Testament materials.

I commend this book as an honest attempt to create an understanding of Scripture. Most church leaders will need to deal with the subject one way or another. The author's hope, and mine, is that readers will work through the material, Bible in hand, seeking to answer the question, "What does God want me to believe and do about this subject?" We will not all agree on all points, but that should not cause us to shy away from healthy inquiry into Scripture.

C. Philip Slate
Professor, author, churchman

Introduction

Another book on women! How could there possibly be a need, given the massive amount of attention this topic has received in the last 50 years since the revival of the women's movement in the West? Although several reasons can be cited, the short answer is that in the Churches of Christ in North America we have reached a dangerous impasse on this subject. The rift that has resulted threatens to become an unbridgeable chasm that imperils our unity, as once again we have allowed ourselves to become swamped by another "issue." So, this book has been written to engage fellow members of the Churches of Christ in a fresh consideration of whether or not limitations on women that are common in most of our congregations rest on a firm biblical base.

The impetus for the book came from the groundbreaking book, *God's Woman*, written in 1938 by the respected evangelist, educator, writer, and debater, C. R. Nichol. Nichol was troubled by what he believed to be unbiblical limitations on women in the church, especially on their teaching men in group settings. Breaking with traditional interpretations, he did a fresh study of the Bible in which he arrived at some conclusions that troubled certain of his contemporaries. Others, including his friend, N. B. Hardeman, applauded his work, stating that it would become a textbook at his college. In the decades to follow, the influence of *God's Woman* waned, and those favoring the more traditional limitations on women in the church prevailed. With the coming of the women's movement in the last third of the twentieth century, positions and practices in certain portions of the Churches of Christ in North America have even hardened.

This book is an effort to try again what Nichol attempted to do decades ago. Like *God's Woman*, it seeks to peel away layers of tradition and examine the relevant biblical passages, avoiding as much as possible the overlay of both tradition and modern concepts. In the spirit of our commitment to the principle that our practice be governed by what we find in the Bible, this book will attempt to draw its conclusions only from what the Bible actually says, rather than what its interpreters think it implies. It will then attempt to apply generally accepted best practices in interpretation to those biblical statements. The goal is to shed some new light that will help bring us closer together in our understanding of the way we should be treating women in the church.

Timeliness of This Topic

CHANGE IS DIFFICULT. MOST OF US ARE CONSERVATIVE AT heart in the sense that our natural reaction to change is to resist. We need to be convinced that the need for change is compelling enough to get us out of our comfort zone. This is doubly the case when it comes to matters of our religious faith. We require reassurance that any change does not go against God's will, since we measure our beliefs and practices against our understanding of that will as revealed in the Bible. This is particularly the case when we feel the pressure of the world around us urging us in a direction that is new to us. We rightly feel compelled to stand our ground on what we believe the Bible teaches. However, sometimes that urging from our culture turns out to be right and we have been behind the curve, as in the case of race relations in many of our congregations and Christian colleges. This book is being written in the conviction that another of those moments in our history has arrived. Just as with race relations, where reexamination of the Scriptures on the topic, though prompted in part from external influences, was what led to needed change, the same "back to the Bible" stance must characterize us as we respond to external pressures on our practice concerning women in the church. The costs of getting this one wrong are so great that avoiding a serious reexamination of what the Scriptures say on women in the church does not seem to be a safe option any longer. If we or any other individuals or churches who also have a high view of Scripture have been wrong in the way we have limited our sisters in their participation in the work and worship of the church, consider these four consequences of continuing to do so.

Alienating Our Young People. As we have all noticed, large numbers of our young people have moved on. They are casualties of the culture wars raging in our society. Many a young Christian woman has lamented the fact that the only place in her world where she has restrictions placed on her because of her gender is the church. Large numbers of our young Christian men feel her hurt and likewise are becoming estranged from the faith of their parents. As a campus minister for twenty years, I saw this type of estrangement happen over and over as young people tasted the freedom that college offered. Thankfully, many of them later came back to the Lord and the church because they reconnected with the values and beliefs that had been instilled in them earlier in life. However, it is different this time. What they see as unjustified discrimination against women runs counter to the values they now so firmly hold. If we have been right on women in the church, of course we should hold the line.

But if we are wrong on this one, we run the enormous risk of pushing our young people away, unnecessarily. We must make sure we get this one right!

Alienating Our Culture. Historically, the teachings of Christ have been the impetus for virtually all the improvements in morality and ethical treatment of others in Western culture. On the matter of women in the church, however, the traditional Christian practices are seen in our culture as archaic and oppressive. This current culture views itself as taking the higher road and we the lower. They see themselves as our ethical superiors, so our influence on them has been weakened significantly. Again, if they are wrong, we should not flinch in staying our course, but if they are right, we are doing inestimable, unnecessary damage to our ability to reach them with the gospel. We must make sure we get this one right!

Failure to Use Many of the Gifts of Half of Our Members. Many who have written on this subject have understandably resisted the argument that if a person has a gift from God, we should not place restrictions on its use. In countering this, it has been pointed out, I think correctly, that if those restrictions come from God, they override our freedom to exercise them. After all, tongue speakers and prophets were restricted in the use of their gifts in the Corinthian assemblies (I Cor. 14:27-32). But what if the restrictions we have placed on women do not actually come from God, but rather from our *mis*understanding of the relevant biblical passages? In that case, we would be putting restrictions on half of our members that are human and not divine, and we would continue to be much poorer for it. We must make sure we get this one right!

Limiting the Freedom of Half of Our Members. Limiting another's freedom in Christ is a very serious matter (see Gal.

2:4, 5:1). Often the argument is made that when choosing between two courses of action where the proper choice is not clear, we should follow the safer path. I have been an elder in two congregations. For some or all of the time in those congregations we have limited women's participation in the assembly in ways I no longer believe are biblical. Do you think, as one who must give an account for my shepherding (Heb. 13:17), I want to stand before God having wrongly restricted the freedom in Christ of half the members in my congregation? I do not regard that as the safer course. We leaders must make sure we get this one right!

Importance of This Topic

Questionable Assumptions. First, a whole host of problematic assumptions permeate the literature on women in the church. Assumptions are premises that we use to draw other conclusions. We do not feel obligated to support or try to prove them, either because we consider them self-evident or we believe they have been sufficiently established elsewhere. We all make assumptions and reason from them. The problem comes when we allow our assumptions to become fact to such an extent that we are either unaware of them or are unwilling to reconsider them. Here are a few of the questionable assumptions about the teaching of the biblical text relating to women in the church that will be addressed in this book.

- God made man (Adam) a protector of woman (Eve).

- The concept of male spiritual leadership is found in the Genesis creation narrative.

- The teachings of Genesis 2-3 apply to men and women in general, rather than to husband and wife.

- The wife's submission to her husband as found in Gen. 3:16 was later transferred to women's submission to men in the church.

- Leading is by its very nature domineering or a lack of submission.

- Teaching by its very nature has authority attached to it.

- Serving in some capacity in the assembly is assuming an unbiblical leadership role.

- Women in general are to be in submission to men in general in the church.

- Gal. 3:28 is Paul's Magna Carta for women and is primary to any other Pauline texts on women.

Inconsistencies. Second, in writings on women in the church, several inconsistencies appear and need to be noted:

- How is it that the creation story in Genesis 2-3 is interpreted as supporting the subordination of women to men in general or in the church when the chapters are clearly discussing the husband-wife relationship?

- How is it that women are prevented from praying out loud in the assembly based simply on an *inference* in I Tim. 2:8-10 when the *clear teaching* of I Cor. 11:5 is that they did so in the Corinthian assemblies?

- How is it that some use the reference to the creation story in I Tim. 2:13-14 to insist that I Tim. 2:12 applies the same way today as it did in first-century Ephesus, but they do not interpret the reference to the creation in I Cor. 11:8-9 as requiring women to wear a head covering today?

- How is it that some take almost all of the 40 verses of I Corinthians 14 as not being applicable today but insist that two verses (34-35) are?

Keeping the Bible at the Center. Much of the discussion among us and the rest of the biblically-focused Christian world has either been a reiteration of traditional interpretations or a nod to our culture. Too often a study of the relevant biblical texts in their own contexts, done without the pressure applied by either of these two influences, has languished in the background. This book is an attempt to examine these passages in the belief that according to our Restoration heritage, serious biblical interpretive work is the best, indeed the only, way to provide the true foundation we need for determining current practice in our modern setting.

Practical Matters

Target Audience. This book has been written primarily for the serious, intelligent, non-specialist whose approach to the Bible is still more one of wonder and a desire to learn than it is to find evidence to support what he/she already believes.

Approach. Because this book has been written within a fellowship that like many in the Christian world at large has a high view of Scripture, it is basically an exegetical study of the relevant biblical passages relating to women in the church. It challenges the serious Bible student to reopen the topic of what women may do in worship assemblies and beyond. This is done by providing a fresh examination of relevant biblical passages without the baggage of centuries of unquestioned interpretations or the contamination of reading our world into that of the Bible.

Flow of the Chapters. The first three chapters form the basis for the rest of the book by examining the way some Christians have used the Bible to support a plethora of conflicting views on women in the church and by proposing a healthier exegetical framework that is used throughout the rest of the book in interpreting the relevant passages. Then the part of the book that examines the relevant biblical passages (chapters four through eleven) begins with the creation narrative, moves next to Jesus and finally to Paul. The last chapter then attempts to pull it all together.

Discussion Questions

1. Which of the items on the author's list of "Questionable Assumptions" match assumptions you have made?

2. Do any of the four "Inconsistencies" the author identifies seem inconsistent to you as well?

3. What do you think the young people in your congregation believe about the limitations generally placed on women in the church?

4. Where else in our culture are women as limited in what they may do as they are in your congregation?

CHAPTER ONE

God's Woman

There is a common misconception among many in the Churches of Christ that the move to broaden the participation of women in congregational assemblies is rather recent. The assumption is that this development flows more from the influence of popular culture than a commitment to Scripture as our guide in religious matters. This book will seek to correct that misconception. Actually, significant challenges to the traditional limitation on women's roles in Christian assemblies were issued decades ago by highly respected Bible students based on serious examination of the relevant biblical passages. Perhaps most notable among these is *God's Woman* written in 1938 by C. R. Nichol.

C.R. Nichol

NICHOL WAS WELL RESPECTED BY HIS PEERS BOTH FOR HIS grasp of the Scriptures and his dedication to his religious heritage. He served for decades as an educator, evangelist, writer, and especially debater. In fact, he held his first debate at age 22, and by the time he was 28 years old he had already conducted 60 of his more than 350 religious debates. In his death notice in the *Firm Foundation*, Reuel Lemmons wrote, "We seriously doubt whether any man since Alexander Campbell has so influenced the destiny of the church in America" (1961, p. 450). At the 2004

Freed-Hardeman University lectures Nobel Patterson called Nichol "one of the most important and influential figures in the growth of New Testament Christianity of the past 125 years." Finally, in 1938 in the *Gospel Advocate* N. B. Hardeman not only endorsed the content of *God's Woman*, he stated that "this book will serve as a text at Freed-Hardeman College" (p. 992).

God's Woman

WHILE *GOD'S WOMAN* ADDRESSES MANY ISSUES RELATING to women in the Bible, reduced to its most basic point it contends that the Bible does not in either the Old or the New Testament forbid women to teach men. What she is not allowed to do is usurp authority over men or fail to be subordinate to them. So, when she teaches men in a way that she remains subordinate to them she is following God's design. A statement in his chapter on "Women at Work" will suffice to illustrate the boldness of his claim.

> In Old Testament times men went to women for instructions, and God inspired women to impart the instruction and information the men needed. Women *must not* usurp authority over the man in the meeting house, the store, the automobile, or on the field of battle. But there have been conditions under which woman taught a group of men, including high priest, by God's authority, without usurping authority over man, and she can do the same today (p. 47).

What follows is a synopsis of Nichol's key points as he progresses through the book.

Women Teachers/Leaders in the Bible

IN THE OLD TESTAMENT, NICHOL POINTED TO MIRIAM (Ex. 15:20; Micah 6:4), Deborah (Judg. 4:4-14; 5:7) and Huldah (II Ki. 22:14-20; II Chron. 34:22-28) as examples of women who taught and/or led men. Miriam was the first prophetess in the Old Testament. Of Deborah he wrote, "Deborah. . . was at the time Judge in Israel; and she was also a prophetess (Judges 4:4-14; 5:7). She served not only in religious affairs, but in civil matters also. She was a prophetess and communicated God's will to the people" (p. 24). He further saw Deborah as an example of "the fact that teaching and helping a man in any work assigned him by Jehovah, is not usurping authority over man; nor do women in such work fail to show themselves to be in subjection to man" (p. 26). From Huldah's example he is even more direct:

> A woman can teach a group of men, even the men who occupied the highest positions in the land, without usurping authority over them. Surely if a woman can teach people things pertaining to the destiny of nations, without usurping authority over them, she can teach men about the destiny of their souls without usurping authority over them! If within the heart of any one there arises the question of the righteousness of the course of Huldah teaching the group of men, let it be remembered that she was inspired by Jehovah to do the teaching! God does not inspire people to do wrong (p. 28).

In applying this to today, Nichol concluded, "This woman, Huldah, taught a group of men without usurping authority over them, and women can teach men today without refusing to be in subjection to men" (p. 30).

In the New Testament he singled out as examples the prophetess Anna (Luke 2:36), the deaconess Phoebe (Rom. 16:1), Priscilla (taught a man – Acts 18:26), women helpers in Philippi (Acts 16; Phil. 4:2-3), and Philip's daughters (Acts 21:9). He further noted that "It is a matter of Old Testament prophecy that women would be teachers in the New Testament times; and it is a matter or [*sic*] record in the New Testament that they did teach (Joel 2; Acts 2; 21:9, I Cor. 11)" (pp. 30-31, 45).

The Dress of Women

IN THE FIRST OF HIS CHAPTERS DEALING WITH SUBJEC-tion, Nichol concludes that custom alone, not God, dictates women's hair length and adornment and their head covering. As far as men's hair length is concerned, it comes down to custom as well. "There is no legislation on the actual length of the hair by Jehovah. Legislation on the style of dressing the hair is not found in God's word" (p. 59).

Subjection

IN THIS CHAPTER NICHOL RECOGNIZES THAT IN THE REAL world of families the husband may not be as fit to lead the family as his wife. He offers two possible courses of action for the wife. First, "under such lamentable conditions it most needs be that the wife strive to lead through the hus-band—that she steer him and the children into proper paths." Secondly, a more extreme deficiency in the husband may call for a more extreme response by the wife. "Not infrequently the wife outranks the husband in every desirable thing, except physical strength. When such conditions exist, if the family functions to its best interest, and proves itself to be a godsend to society it may be necessary to ignore the lead of the husband" (p. 88).

Within the confines of the husband's overall leadership of the wife, Nichol strongly emphasizes mutuality in the way the home is run. He sees both the husband and the wife as ruling the home.

> The divine order is that the husband rule the household, and too, it is the order of heaven that the *wife* rule the household. In the home it is not "one man rule." Together the husband and wife build the home, and jointly they are to direct the affairs of the home; rearing the children and in an orderly manner conducting the discipline and details necessary in all things pertaining to the home (p. 100).

Nichol even applies mutual subjection to the home. In commenting on Eph. 5:21, he writes, "But we are to be in 'subjection to one another,' that is, have regard for the rights of others, seek to serve others. In the same way the wife is to be in 'subjection' to her husband, and the husband is to be in 'subjection' to the wife" (p. 110).

I Corinthians 11:4-5

Nichol sees the matter of women's head covering and hair length as simply Corinthian custom and nothing to do with what is right or wrong per se (p. 120). On women praying he opposes the idea advanced by some that (1) women were praying silently and/or (2) were only to do it privately. On the first he shows the inconsistency of claiming silent prayer, when the same cannot be said of prophesying. As to the second point, he argues that the distinction between public and private activities in worship is not biblical. Concluding that the argument that women were only allowed to pray out loud in private comes from a misinterpretation of I Cor. 14:34-35 about women's silence, he asserts that in neither I Corinthians 14 "or in any other inspired statement" is there "a prohibition against women speaking in public, *on the ground that it is public*" (pp. 121-23).

I Corinthians 14:34-35

NICHOL IS QUITE FORCEFUL IN HIS DENIAL THAT THE ASSEMBLY being discussed in I Corinthians 14 has anything to do with today. It is giving instructions for assemblies where spiritual gifts were being exercised, and since those assemblies do not exist today, the passage offers no instructions for our day. Thus, he rejects any attempt by people today to use I Cor. 14:34-35 to limit what women may do in the assembly, including forbidding women to pray out loud in the assembly (p. 121).

I Timothy 2:8-14

FOR NICHOL THIS PASSAGE IS CRUCIAL. THE CENTRAL message of his whole book is correcting what he regarded as a common misunderstanding of the prohibition of women's teaching in 2:12. He argues forcefully that the passage does not prevent women from praying in the presence of men or teaching them. First, he asserts that the fact that men are directed to pray (2:8) does not imply that women are not to pray (p. 146). As far as teaching is concerned, he believes he has proven that women may teach men in all sorts of settings, so the prohibition in 2:12 has to do with the *manner* in which they teach men. Finally, since the key point is that women are to be in subjection to men, how would they be considered in subjection if they were capable of giving a man information but refused (p. 151).

The Deaconess

NICHOL BELIEVES THE "WOMEN" IN I TIM. 3:11 WERE deaconesses, not wives of the deacons, reasoning that

> It seems absurd to contend that Paul when discussing the qualifications of a deacon would turn aside abruptly and mention the character of the deacon's wife; but makes no reference to the character of the bishop's wife, when in the same connection he had discussed the qualifications of bishops, but did not say one word about the qualifications of the bishop's wife (p. 161).

God's Woman's Reception

IN *GOD'S WOMAN* NICHOL FOUND HIMSELF AT ODDS WITH David Lipscomb, his esteemed teacher at Nashville Bible School. Earlier some of Lipscomb's views on women in the church and those of Nichol were more compatible, but by the time Nichol attended the school in Nashville, Lipscomb's position had hardened somewhat. In some respects, Nichol was reclaiming old territory that had been lost. In others he was breaking new ground. G. C. Brewer, in an article written only four years before the publication of *God's Woman*, noted that earlier in his life he had heard women pray publicly, a practice no longer common. He questioned whether some of the restrictions on women's participation in worship had become custom and perhaps should be reexamined. This is exactly what *God's Woman* did.

The book received a mixed reception when it was first published. John T. Lewis was quick to oppose it, accusing Nichol of being motivated by the desire to please the women in the church, an accusation that severely hurt Nichol. Perhaps the most notable criticism came only a few months later from Nichol's close friend, Foy E. Wallace Jr., who stated that the church would have been better off if the book had never been written. It also received enthusiastic endorsements. M. O. Daley stated in the Introduction that "'God's Woman' is not 'just another book,' but is one, which in its field of endeavor, and the character of its content, will 'fill a long felt want' in the prayerful study of God's word" (p. 11). In a publication notice imbedded in W. E. Brightwell's "News and Notes" in the Nov. 3, 1938 issue of the *Gospel Advocate*, he wrote further,

> "God's Woman," a new book, by C. R. Nichol, is a pains-taking search of the Bible to learn all the truth about woman's work under God. I know of no book that so thoroughly covers the subject. False doctrine is exposed, and the truth is made to stand out. The arrangement for class work adds much to its value. I predict for the book a hearty welcome, and a wide circulation (p. 1040).

Probably the most notable and enthusiastic endorsement came in the same section of the journal two weeks earlier. N. B. Hardeman, President of Freed-Hardeman College, wrote,

> I have read carefully 'God's Woman.' This is a most thor-ough discussion of what the Bible says about women. The arguments are clear, logical. The author does not evade such difficult passages as 1 Cor. 14:34, 35 and 1 Tim. 2:11, 12. He does not share the opinions held by many commentaries. I verily believe he has gone to the heart of what Paul had in mind and brought forth the truth. This book will serve as a text in Freed-Hardeman College. I commend the book to all interested in learning about 'God's Woman' (p. 992).

Other Voices of Dissent

Lest it be assumed that Nichol was alone in dis-senting from some of the traditional limitations that have been placed on women in the church, here is a sampling of dissenting interpretations of those who wrote before the latest woman's movement in the last third of the twentieth century. They have been chosen because their views were not influenced in any way by the recent changes in our culture.

Women prayed and prophesied out loud outside the assembly when men were present. (David Lipscomb)

Women prayed out loud in the regular assemblies. (Moses Lard)

Women prophesied in the regular assemblies. (J. W. McGarvey)

I Cor. 11:3-16 refers to the regular congregational assembly. (McGarvey, J. W. Roberts, Guy N. Woods)

I Cor. 11:3-16 is primarily concerned with the wife's subjection to her husband (not to men and women in general). (McGarvey, Clarence C. Gobbel, Roberts)

The headship of man in I Cor. 11:3 refers to the husband's headship of his wife (not to men and women in general). (Roberts)

I Cor. 14:34-35 states the rule for women's silence in the assembly, but the rule had exceptions in the first century (e.g., I Cor. 11:5), and it does today. (McGarvey)

The women in I Cor. 14:34-35 were wives with Christian husbands. (J. W. Chism, George W. DeHoff)

Women's not speaking in I Cor. 14:34-35 refers to their not dictating to or usurping authority over men, not absolute silence. (J. C. McQuiddy)

According to I Cor. 14:34-35, women may teach in the assembly, as long as they do not usurp authority over a man. (DeHoff)

I Cor. 14:34-35 may refer only to Greek churches, like those in Corinth and Ephesus. (B. W. Johnson)

Since spiritual gifts were being exercised there, the type of assembly reflected in I Cor. 14:34-35 does not exist today. (DeHoff)

Only the customs of the age made it shameful for a woman to speak in church (I Cor. 14:35). That is no longer the case. (McGarvey)

Women may teach in a way that does not usurp authority over a man and fulfil the requirements of I Tim. 2:11-12. (Dehoff)

Women are free to teach men in private, and this includes teaching a class in the meeting house, as long as others are doing it as well. (Lipscomb)

On the matter of whether the first-century church had female deacons in a formal ministry alongside their male counterparts, for the most part, the leaders of the Restoration Movement in the nineteenth century, beginning with Alexander Campbell himself, were uniform in their answer in the affirmative. G. C. Brewer in the twentieth century can be added to their number.

A Way Forward

AT THE VERY LEAST, THESE EXAMPLES DEMONSTRATE THAT serious Bible students in past generations have come to vastly different conclusions from the hardened ones today. They wrote decades before the social change brought about by the women's movement and other factors in the last third of the twentieth century. Their conclusions can hardly be attributed to these societal forces.

In his own chapter at the end of *God's Woman*, M. O. Daley speaks about how we are so indebted in our knowledge of the Bible to what we have learned from those who have gone before. In a sense, we all stand on the shoulders of former students of the Bible. They have taught us what they have learned so we can begin at that point and learn even more. So it is with *God's Woman*. On certain key points my own study diverges from Nichol's understanding, but many of the conclusions of the book have provided a starting point for further study. What a pity it is that what Nichol and others have to teach us has somehow gotten lost, leaving us to wrestle with questions decades later as if some of the answers being given today were somehow new.

This present study is a revisiting of *God's Woman* as a reminder that some of its conclusions are not new. That ground was broken more than 80 years ago, and we need to acknowledge with gratitude and affection the one who did it. Standing on the shoulders of Nichol and others, I propose to do exactly what he did. This book reflects fresh study of the Scriptures over the course of many years. Though the conclusions are mine, the debt I owe to others for their help in reaching them is immense.

Discussion Questions

1. Why do you think the author begins his study of the biblical passages relating to women in the church with C. R. Nichol's book?

2. Have you ever suspected that something your parents or a respected teacher at church taught you was wrong? How did that feel and how did you deal with it?

3. Do any of Nichol's points that go against the flow of what the church typically teaches or practices make sense to you? Which ones?

4. How can we balance respect for what the church has always taught—on any subject—with the need to take a fresh look at what the Bible actually teaches?

CHAPTER TWO

The Current Impasse

C hapter one detailed some of the significant challenges to the traditional teachings on women in the church that occurred before the women's movement in the last third of the twentieth century. This chapter will begin by examining the great diversity of opinions among writers who oppose widening the participation of women in our assemblies. It will then consider the question of why we have been unable to agree on our understanding of the key biblical passages.

Lack of Consensus

STUDIES IN OUR BROTHERHOOD ON THE TOPIC OF WOMEN in the church are a vast wasteland. Interpretations are all over the place, and this is not limited to one side or the other on this whole topic. For a fellowship that prides itself in "speaking where the Bible speaks and being silent where the Bible is silent" and "calling Bible things by Bible names," lapses on this subject are far too common. There is the invention of terminology or concepts not found in the text and their use as evidence for conclusions drawn later. There is the proof texting of verses like Gal. 3:28 or I Cor. 14:34a, pushing them far beyond the bounds of their context and reading into them ideas not found in the text. There are arguments more at home with the methodology of modern Sociology than with serious biblical criticism. There is the reading of modern church practices into the New Testament (NT) period as if they were present among the first-century Christians. There is what can only be described as careless or at least highly suspect interpretation of relevant Old Testament (OT) passages. And the list goes on.

But possibly the most troublesome has been the enormous diversity of opinions coupled with the confident assertion of the interpreters that *their* understanding is the one that is most faithful to the biblical text. How can the same Bible be the source of such contradictory views if we are simply letting the Bible speak to us? Perhaps some of our methods of Bible study are flawed. Or is it possible that sometimes what we get out of a text is more influenced by what we bring to it than what we find in it? Maybe we have held to some conclusions so long that we find it difficult truly to look at a passage with fresh eyes.

Many would have us believe that what a woman may or may not do in the assembly and other gatherings of Christians is crystal clear in the NT. Yet, these interpreters cannot agree among themselves. Although numerous instances could be produced, here is just one example of significant disagreement over the settings to which the three key Pauline passages on women in the church were written, culled from writings of authors in the Churches of Christ who favor the traditional limitations on women in the church:

I Corinthians 11:3-16. The type of assemblies where women were praying and prophesying was (1) the regular congregational assemblies, (2) house church meetings, or (3) non-regular public assemblies where men were present.

I Corinthians 14:33b-35. The restriction on women speaking in church refers (1) only to the regular Christian assembly or (2) only to special assemblies where miraculous gifts were being used.

I Timothy 2:8-15. On the meaning of "in every place" (2:8) where some interpreters assume that women are excluded from praying: (1) the assembly only, (2) any situation, public or private, where men are present, (3) religious assemblies only where men are present, (4) includes devotionals where teenage boys are present, (5) includes at home where wives may not pray in the presence of their husbands and sons and daughters may not pray in the presence of their fathers or brothers, (6) includes even one woman in the presence of one man, (7) includes older Christian women praying with Christian boys present, or (8) women leading prayer in the presence of *adult* males.

Such disarray among Bible students who presumably believe that what they are writing is correct because they are faithfully representing the Bible can lead only to the conclusion that this is not a matter that is as cut and dried as some try to present it. It is time to exercise a little more humility, a lot more discipline in our Bible study, and more charity toward each other.

Why So Much Disagreement?

WHY IS IT THAT WE DISAGREE SO MUCH ON HOW WE understand and apply biblical passages? It is not because truth is unknowable or is not objective. More constructive is the recognition that, while much of the Bible is rather straightforward and easy to understand, some passages are simply difficult. Our disappointing track record on interpretation of passages on women in the church is ample evidence that this is one of the more difficult issues to understand. But why are some passages so difficult that we have trouble coming to agreement on their meaning?

Some Reasons for Disagreements

Reasons Beyond the Interpreter's Control

Some Passages Are Inherently Difficult to Understand.
Peter even said that about some of Paul's writings (II Pet. 3:16). In the vast majority of cases, though, the meaning is plain and straightforward, even 2,000 years later. However, probably about five to ten percent of the passages are particularly difficult to understand. Unfortunately for us, most of the NT texts dealing with women in the church come from Paul and fall into that five to ten percent.

The Original Readers Had Some Obvious Advantages We Do Not Have. Compared with the original readers, we have a knowledge deficiency. Our disadvantage in understanding the NT is in our distance in time from the world in which it was written and originally read. Among other things, this limited familiarity with their world has to do with language, culture, and common experience.

Language. The NT was written in the Greek of the Hellenistic Period. More than any other time in history we are blessed with wonderful translations and tools for understanding what the original Greek meant. But no living person has the Greek of the period of the NT as his or her native language. The best we can do is study it from a distance. Most of the time the translations are clear enough and the texts straightforward enough that those who know Greek have no advantage over those who do not. However, sometimes the greatest of Greek scholars have to throw up their hands and say, "This is the best I can do for now, but I don't know for sure." We can never completely overcome the disadvantage of not sharing a common language with the first-century Christians.

Culture. Consider the example of the women and men's head coverings in I Corinthians 11. When the Corinthians read this they understood instantly what Paul meant. It was a part of their culture, their experience, their world. Many statements in the NT that the original readers understood readily are obscure to us because we live in a different time and culture. We can minimize this disadvantage through study, but we can never completely overcome it.

Common Experience. Somewhat related to the above, especially in the NT letters, the writer and the recipients shared a common experience. Thus, the Corinthians would know which of the issues Paul addresses were on their list of questions to him (I Cor. 7:1). Further, they would know what he wrote in the previous letter he alludes to in I Cor. 5:9. We can never completely overcome the disadvantage of not sharing their common experience.

Lest the impression be left that the first-century Christians had all the advantages and we have none, we should acknowledge one huge advantage we have over them. We have the entire NT, and it is readily available to us. They had only bits and pieces, a letter here, a gospel there. The ability to mass produce written material brought about by the invention of printing makes the Bible so much more accessible to us than to them. It is hard to overemphasize how significant this advantage is for our ability to do serious study of God's word.

Reasons Within the Interpreter's Control

MORE OFTEN THAN WE WOULD LIKE TO ADMIT, *WE* ARE the obstacle to properly understanding the Bible. This has been particularly the case on the topic of women in the church. It has become such a lightning-rod issue that we often do not apply the same careful methods of Bible study to these passages that we do to others. We may lower our standards of biblical interpretation, because we feel so strongly about our understanding, and its "truthfulness" is so self-evident to us. The result is that our methodology for approaching the biblical text and understanding it is sometimes flawed. Lest anyone think I am pointing my finger at others who do these things without realizing that I, too, have been guilty, let me give myself as an example of this careless use of the Bible.

When Pat and I got married, it was common for the bride's vows to include, "love, honor and obey." Pat's brother, who performed our ceremony, wanted to remove the word "obey" from the vows, but I held firm that I thought it should be there. It was not that I had any interest in ordering Pat around in our marriage or in requiring her obedience. It was because I believed that Paul's words to Christian wives in Eph. 5:22-24 should not be watered down simply because our society at the time seemed to be pushing us in that direction. Then for many years I used the word "obey" in the vows of weddings I performed. I was certain that I was on firm biblical ground in this and did not even consider that I might be wrong. Many years later I read an article on Eph. 5:21-6:9 in which the author pointed out that children and slaves were required to "obey," but not wives. I was horrified that I was so wrong and so careless as to import into Eph. 5:22-24 an element found in the other two passages but not there. I had made up something that was not in the text, in my mind had inserted it into the text, and had patterned my erroneous practice on this fabrication. There is enough of this sort of thing going on in all of us that it should both humble us and cause us to rededicate ourselves to the careful, disciplined type of Bible study we know we should be doing all the time.

Flawed Methodology

IF WE APPROACH THE BIBLICAL TEXT WITH FAULTY ASSUMPtions, closed minds, or questionable methods of interpretation, the quality of the result is doomed from the start. What follows are some of the more common types of flawed methodology drawn from publications within the Churches of Christ.

1. **Proof Texting**. One of the quickest ways to misuse or misconstrue a statement is to separate it from its context. Proof texting involves taking a statement out of its context and applying it to another setting in a way that is either inconsistent with its meaning in the original context or does not account for the differences between the two contexts. As mentioned earlier, many who write on this subject are guilty of proof texting Gal. 3:28 or I Cor. 14:34a. This book will later deal with these two texts in some detail in their contexts.

2. **Failure to Take Proper Account of the Context**. This is closely related to proof texting, but interprets a statement without due consideration of its literary (the text of the Bible in which the statement is situated) and historical (the setting to which the statement is addressed) contexts. One example is the assertion by one writer that "the Law" in I Cor. 14:34 refers to anywhere in the OT. He then uses I Sam. 2:1-10 to demonstrate that "the Law" provides an example of a woman praying in the presence of a man. The context, however, shows that Paul's reference to "the Law" here is meant to *restrict*, not permit these wives' actions.

3. **Uncritical Use of Background Evidence**. A common
mistake is to take a piece of evidence from background
material, such as a quote of a Greek or Roman author, and
apply it uncritically to a specific situation discussed in the
NT as if it were the precise background against which a
NT author wrote. It is uncritical because it fails to take
proper account of such factors as (1) the actual *context* of
the statement, (2) *provenance* in time and place, and (3)
how *representative* the statement is of ancient views on the
subject it is addressing. It is a common failing of those who
have a limited acquaintance with the primary sources in
question, but unfortunately, any of us can fall into this trap.

An example of the uncritical use of Rabbinic background
material on women is the oft-repeated statement by Rabbi
Eliezer that "whoever gives his daughter a knowledge of
the Law it is as though he taught her lasciviousness." This
citation is frequently used as *representative* of the Rabbinic
attitude toward women at the time of Jesus and Paul.
For several years I did so myself, until I actually read the
words in *context*. Out of context, the comment sounds
absolute, but in context it is clear that the speaker had a
limited situation in mind. This tractate (chapter) of the
Mishnah (*Sotah*) deals exclusively with the interpretation
of Num. 5:11-31, where a wife is suspected of adultery. R.
Eliezer is talking about a woman who has been charged
with adultery who seeks to use this passage in the Torah in
her defense. In this case, to teach a daughter this specific
law would be to give her the ability to escape the full
consequences of her sexual sin, so the father might as
well teach her lasciviousness. Obviously the quotation has
nothing to do with the general Rabbinic attitude toward
women, but with a specific issue.

4. **Uncritical Use of Lexical Tools**. Dealing with the language of the Bible is tricky, because words have multiple meanings. Lexicons or dictionaries of NT words are excellent tools, but for the serious Bible student, nothing is more useful than a good concordance. How we use these tools, though, is key to getting a good result. For instance, using an English dictionary to define a word in an English translation can lead to invalid conclusions. How could anyone possibly understand the correct meaning of the Greek words behind the English word "church" or "baptism" or "saint" by using an English dictionary?

One of the most common uncritical approaches to determining the meaning of a Greek word in a specific passage is to pick one of several possible meanings in a Greek lexicon and assert without further evidence that it is *the* proper meaning in the passage at hand. For example, one expositor used Thayer's lexicon to define the meaning of the Greek word for "teach" (*didaskō*) in I Tim. 2:12 as "deliver didactic discourses." Although this is only one of about ten shades of meaning Thayer gives for the word, it became useful for the writer to single out this one because the word "discourse" in the definition enabled him to make the leap that Paul is talking about preaching as well as teaching in the passage. This is why serious Bible students should use a concordance to supplement the views expressed in lexicons. Concordance study allows us to test our own conclusions about specific word meanings against those of a lexicographer.

5. **Demonizing Those Who Disagree**. This is a particularly destructive activity, and we ought to know better. It has to do with pushing or crossing the line between attacking a brother's position and attacking the brother himself. For

example, one author in an article on women in the church in describing a person's disagreement with a point he was making wrote that it was "selfish, arrogant, and illustrates the damnable 'will worship' loathed by the Almighty." He is not alone in calling others arrogant. Another wrote, "If there is a unifying spirit that characterizes the new 'left wing' of the current church, it is that of arrogance." On the other side, one writer characterized Christian men who hold the traditional view on women in the church as "so enraptured with their authority, so enamored of their self-serving responsibility, so blinded by their insecurity, so weakened by their shallow love." Whether or not these descriptors are accurate is irrelevant in determining the validity of the points made by those to whom they are applied. Statements are true or false, regardless of who makes them. We see enough of this kind of speech in political rhetoric. We don't need it in the church. Surely there is "still a more excellent way" (I Cor. 12:31b).

6. **Reading Elements into the Text That Are Not There**. This is done in various ways. One is what some call *eisegesis*, as opposed to *exegesis*. While exegesis involves extracting the original meaning from a text, eisegesis has to do with introducing to the text issues not found there. Another is the failure to approach a passage with as open a mind as possible. Rather, we saddle the text with preconceptions that inhibit discovery of a passage's meaning. Finally, some writers are actually guilty of manufacturing ideas and concepts not found in the text and treating them as if they were. Consider the following:

Interjecting Modern Ideas and Experiences. One example is the practice of interpreting both OT and NT texts on the relationship between men and women within the framework of modern Sociology. Words like "patriarchy," "matriarchy," "egalitarian," or "complementary" are thrown around as if they were in the Bible. Modern positions on the issue are characterized by such descriptors as "Evangelical Feminism," "Patriarchalism," or "Hierarchal Complementarianism." Those whose approaches are so labeled can then be safely put away in a box and their conclusions on individual biblical passages dismissed. It is not that using the theories of modern Sociology or any of the other social sciences is without value. For some people these theories help bring into focus the *application* of biblical texts to our present situation. It is their interjection into the investigation of the *original* meaning of biblical passages where they can become anachronistic impediments to our understanding. We should allow the Bible to unfold its meaning to us before we start applying more recent post-biblical concepts to it.

Interjecting Presuppositions. Presuppositions or assumptions are the premises we use to draw other conclusions. We do not feel obligated to support or try to prove them either because we consider them self-evident or we believe they have been sufficiently established elsewhere. That the Bible is the inspired word of God or that Jesus died on the cross to save us from our sins are assumptions we all make. They are assumptions because we are so certain of them that we feel no need to support them by reasoning or evidence. They become the foundation upon which we build other conclusions. Where these presuppositions get us into trouble is when they have no biblical text that supports them. Previously we may have made an effort to establish them by stringing together a gaggle of Bible verses into a reasoned argument or even by making an argument without direct support of biblical texts, but no actual biblical passage supports them. They then become the premises upon which we base other reasoned arguments. Writings on women in the church are filled with these types of unproven or even unprovable assumptions. This book will challenge many of them.

Inventing Terminology and Concepts. Possibly most disappointing of all is the practice of making things up as if they were in the Bible. It is disappointing because this comes from people who pride themselves in not adding to or taking away from the Bible. For example, into the interpretation of the Genesis creation narrative some have inserted concepts like "male spiritual leadership" or Adam as Eve's "designated spiritual protector." Then there is the complete fabrication that one of Adam's two sins was "failing to exercise spiritual leadership." Moving to the NT, one writer asserts that "First Timothy 2:8 forbids women to pray audibly *in the presence* of men in religious assemblies." Note the three foreign elements he adds to the text: (1) "forbids" (the only thing forbidden in the verse is anger and arguing, and that pertains to men, not women); (2) "women" (the verse is talking only about men, not women); and (3) "in the presence of men" (nothing in this verse or in the next two, where women are actually talked about, is said about the presence of men). This is all made up. It is no wonder that there is such great disagreement on what the Bible says about women when so much of the discussion centers on what is not even in the Bible.

7. **Asking Modern Questions of the NT.** In an effort to apply what is found in the NT to our current situation, often people ask modern questions that the NT cannot

answer. For example, "Does God approve of human genetic engineering"? or "Is it a sin for a Christian to smoke cigarettes"? It is not that the NT does not provide us any direction for making decisions on these types of issues. It just does not and cannot give us *specific* direction, because these situations did not exist in the first century or they are not specifically addressed in the NT. On the topic of women in the church these types of questions abound. "May girls pray in mixed devotionals"? "Is it Scriptural for a woman to act as a translator in an assembly"? "May a female pass a communion tray in the assembly"? What we need to remember in dealing with questions like these is that they have to do with the modern-day *application* of NT teachings, not with what specific NT texts actually meant in their original setting.

Conclusions

OUR RECORD IN RESEARCH AND WRITINGS ON WOMEN IN the church has been less than stellar. It is characterized by massive disagreement and sometimes unbrotherly accusations. This is one of those topics where the biblical evidence is difficult and capable of multiple interpretations. It begs the question of whether consensus is possible and if so to what degree. Flawed methodology stands firmly at the center of the differences in our understanding of the relevant biblical passages and their modern application. But this actually offers a ray of hope. If we can identify lapses in our methods, commit ourselves to a more disciplined Bible study, and become more charitable to those with whom we disagree, there is a reasonable expectation we can learn from each other and move closer together. This chapter has dealt primarily with our differences and some of their causes. The next will offer suggestions for what that more disciplined Bible study might look like.

Discussion Questions

1. Were you aware of the scope of disagreement on the role of women in the church by people who claim that their views are supported by the Bible?

2. Have you ever discovered that you had been very wrong in your understanding of a biblical passage? What impact did that realization have on you?

3. Which of the examples of "Flawed Methodology" in biblical studies have you encountered? Can you think of any others?

4. Do you agree with the author in his last paragraph that there is hope that we can achieve greater agreement on the topic of women in the church than has been the case so far? How do we do that?

CHAPTER THREE

What Disciplined Bible Study Looks Like

This chapter will offer suggestions for what a more disciplined Bible study than has often characterized studies on women in the church might look like. First, we will look at what the opposite of the flawed methods discussed in chapter two teaches us about good methodology. After that will be a few suggestions by some in our brotherhood who are widely recognized for their expertise in biblical interpretation and have written books on the topic. Finally, I will propose an approach that pulls all this together.

The Opposite of Flawed Methods

HERE ARE THE TYPES OF FLAWED METHODOLOGY IN BIBLIcal studies mentioned in chapter two and the sound methods their opposite implies.

Awareness of Assumptions

CERTAINLY WE CANNOT TOTALLY FREE OURSELVES OF OUR assumptions or presuppositions, nor should we. We approach the biblical text with certain presuppositions about God and the Bible, and these can and should influence our reading of the text. Where the rub comes is when our presupposi-

tions so close our mind that they prevent our looking at a
passage with fresh eyes. So what are we to do? First, we can
repeatedly remind ourselves that we do not approach the text
as a blank slate, but bring our assumptions, presuppositions
and, on our worst days, prejudices with us. To supplement
this, asking for feedback from someone who disagrees with
our conclusions can provide a needed reality check. Finally,
we can attempt to construct as strong a case as we can for
the contrary view.

Faithfulness to the Context

THE FLAWED METHOD ADDRESSED HERE EXPRESSES ITSELF
in either (1) interpreting a statement or verse out of its context or (2) stringing together individual statements or verses
because of a common thread running through them with
little regard to what they meant in their original contexts.
Two examples from I Cor. 14:34 will suffice. First, what is
the meaning of the word translated "be silent" (*sigaō*) in its
context? A concordance study of how the word is used in
the rest of the chapter would help us here. Or when Paul
uses the word "to speak" (*laleō*), what kind of speaking is he
talking about? Does this refer to speaking of any type (like
speaking while singing, Eph. 5:19) or would a careful look
at the next verse help us reign in some of the speculation
common on this point?

Appropriate Use of Background Evidence

THE MOST COMMON FLAWS IN THIS AREA ARE (1) QUOTING
a pagan or Jewish author out of context, (2) failure to take
proper account of the time and place of a piece of evidence,
and (3) generalizing from a single piece of evidence (Greek,

Roman, Jewish). We must first check the context of a pagan or Jewish quotation to ensure that the author actually meant what we take him to have meant by his isolated statement. Next, since opinions varied widely in the ancient world in different places and times, we must establish the provenance of a statement to assess its relevance to the place and time of the biblical text we are interpreting. Finally, since even in the same general place and time authors' opinions varied widely due to cultural differences and other factors, we must ensure that the evidence is representative enough of the background to illuminate our biblical passage. When it comes to the foreground, that is pagan, Jewish, and Christian sources after the NT, the same principles apply.

Appropriate Use of Lexical Tools

These tools for determining word meanings include Hebrew and Greek concordances and lexicons (dictionaries). They also comprise special word studies found in articles and other books, such as biblical commentaries and theological dictionaries. A concordance and lexicon should be used in tandem. When a word has multiple meanings, we begin by examining usage of the word using a Greek or Hebrew concordance, then validate or modify our findings in a lexicon. If we go into a word study presuming a certain outcome, then use a lexicon to support our presumption, we have reduced significantly the likelihood of getting a correct result.

Chapter two also discussed the methodological flaws of **Reading Elements into the Text That Are Not There** and **Asking Modern Questions of the NT**. The opposite of these will be dealt with in the last section of this chapter.

Suggestions from Authors of Books on Women in the Church

IN SOME OF THE BOOKS ON WOMEN IN THE CHURCH WRITten by a few of our brotherhood's specialists in the field of biblical interpretation, the authors have offered several constructive insights on proper interpretive methodology. What follows is a synopsis of points culled from a few of them. The reader will find certain of their views more useful than others, and there is understandable repetition both from what has been written earlier in this chapter and among these writers themselves. However, their suggestions do have value in helping us consider the way we go about our serious Bible study.

Everett Ferguson

FROM HIS WORK AS A WORLD RENOWNED SPECIALIST ON early Christianity, Ferguson developed a methodology to approach theological issues that he has used at least three times in published works, including in 2003 in his *Women in the Church*. His three-stage approach for sound biblical interpretation is simple and direct.

1. First, he performs an analysis of the relevant biblical texts.

2. Next, he studies the historical context (background) and "the early Christian development after the New Testament" (foreground). "This testimony from history is a control on whether one has read the biblical texts accurately and put them together correctly" (p. 5).

3. Finally, he considers "the doctrinal significance and coherence of the conclusions" that would suggest whether

a practice had ongoing relevance for the church or had meaning primarily in its own cultural setting (pp. 5-6).

Neil R. Lightfoot

IN HIS BOOK, *THE ROLE OF WOMEN: NEW TESTAMENT PERspectives* (1978), Lightfoot summarizes "the exegetical task" as "to gather together the relevant biblical texts, examine them linguistically and contextually, look at them historically, and by this means determine what these texts said to their first readers" (p. 9). To counteract the human element in exegesis he suggests that "the exegete must put himself through a severe test of mind-clearing. Is he willing to put aside his partisan causes and pet ideas?" Finally, in discussing "how to distinguish between culturally-rooted ideas and lasting principles," he admits that there is no magic bullet. The interpreter should just use good common sense (p. 36).

C. R. Nichol

IN HIS BOOK, *GOD'S WOMAN* (1938), NICHOL DOES NOT ADDRESS biblical interpretation as a separate topic, but sprinkled throughout the book are little gems he throws in. There is nothing systematic about his treatment of them, as there is in Ferguson and Lightfoot, but to borrow Lightfoot's term, most can be characterized as "common sense." Here are some of those gems:

- Note the point of emphasis (p. 62).

- Be careful not to put too much weight on what is not said (p. 71).

- Recognize that we do not know some of the background that was fully known to the original recipients (p. 71).

- Let a passage speak for itself (p. 121).
- Not all commands in the Bible apply today (p. 129).
- Consider the circumstances at the time of writing (p. 133).

Carroll D. Osburn

OSBURN FIRST PUBLISHED *WOMEN IN THE CHURCH: REFO-cusing the Discussion* in 1994, then released a greatly expanded second edition in 2001 under the title, *Women in the Church: Reclaiming the Ideal.* Because the latter book contains a fuller treatment of his proposed principles of biblical interpretation, we will follow it in the discussion here. Early in the work he suggests two elements of an approach (p. 4).

1. "Cultivate a willingness to rethink the problem." "Rethinking means that some change might result. So, we must have an honest willingness to change our views and modify our behavior if necessary."

2. "Reexamine the biblical text." We need to do this "instead of rummaging through the Bible to find texts that might support our pre-conceived notions."

Later in the book (p. 104), Osburn argues that "proper biblical interpretation must begin with and be guided by the original, historical, contextual meaning of the text." This means that "the 'meaning' of a text is the meaning intended by the author within a particular literary and historical setting." The rest of Osburn's discussion here is an exceptionally well-structured synopsis of some of the contemporary discussion over how to distinguish the culturally based from the eternal biblical teachings without being overly influenced by our preconceived notions (pp. 104-108). This is so well done that the reader is encouraged to access Osburn's treatment directly, rather than depend on a summary here.

Just as these four writers found it useful to discuss Bible study methodology in their books on women in the church, so it is with this current book. In addition to what has already been said, what follows are some thoughts on a disciplined approach to biblical interpretation in the hope that they will be useful as we move to the relevant texts themselves.

Say, Meant, Mean

IN ORDER TO APPLY BIBLICAL TEACHINGS APPROPRIATELY to our current situation, we need to ask three questions of a biblical text: (1) What does it say?, (2) What did it mean?, and (3) What does it mean? Most studies on biblical hermeneutics stress the importance of the second and third questions, but a failure to pay proper attention to the first often leads interpreters to make statements about what the Bible teaches that are either simply not true or cannot be established from the text itself. Further, these three questions are interconnected, with the second dependent on the first and the third dependent on the first and second. Most of the time we intuitively ask the three questions without being conscious of it. However, in those more difficult texts, where serious Bible students differ among themselves, a more disciplined and intentional use of the three questions is called for.

What Does It Say?

HERE WE ARE CONCERNED WITH (1) ESTABLISHING THE correct reading based on the manuscript evidence and (2) avoiding the confusion about what we think the text meant with what it actually says. Only after we are satisfied that we are interpreting the best reading of the text and have limited ourselves to interpreting what the text actually says are we ready to answer the second question, "What did it mean"?

What Did It Mean?

THIS IS THE *EXEGETICAL* OR *INTERPRETIVE* QUESTION. IT seeks to learn what the original writer actually meant by his words and to a lesser extent how those words would have been understood by his readers. We do this by trying to put ourselves as nearly as possible in the shoes of the original readers, so we can derive the same meaning from a passage that they did. The exegetical question can only be answered correctly once the first question, "What does it say"?, has been addressed. Several factors go into answering this second question, including such things as the

- Original intent of the author and/or speaker
- Various biblical contexts (the passage, the book, the author, the NT, the Bible)
- Meaning of the language used (words, phrases, grammatical constructions)
- Literary form (e.g., parable, hymn, proverb, narrative)
- Historical context (background and foreground).

Unfortunately, if we are not careful, the distinction between the first and second questions can get blurred, such as when an interpreter reads our current situation or modern categories or terminology into a biblical passage. The distinction between the first and second questions can also get blurred when the interpreter makes an assumption about the meaning of a text as if the text actually said that.

For example, on the cross Jesus uttered the words, "My God, my God, why have you forsaken me"? (Matt. 27:46=Mark 15:34). How many sermons have you heard about how the sin of the world on Jesus was so enormous that God had to turn away from him at that moment? The assumption behind that interpretation is that Jesus is crying out in despair in the utter loneliness of that hour. While that is certainly a possible interpretation (second question), that is not what the text actually says (first question). Other interpretations of Jesus' words are possible, and if we assume what the text does not say (that God forsook Jesus in that moment), we may miss what Jesus actually *meant* (second question). Perhaps, for example, Jesus was simply quoting the opening line of Psalm 22, indicating that this Messianic Psalm referred to him. Only after this second question, "What did it mean,"? has been answered are we ready for the third and final one, "What does it mean"?

What Does It Mean?

THIS IS THE *HERMENEUTICAL* OR *APPLICATION* QUESTION. IT seeks to apply what a passage meant (second question) to our specific modern situation. For those of us who believe the Bible is the final authority for our current beliefs and practices, quite often the result of asking the second and third questions will be essentially the same. However, in many cases the results will be different. Simply because a passage meant something in the first century does not mean there is a one-to-one correspondence to our world. Here we consider such factors as

- The original intent of the author and/or speaker
- The basis or reason for the author and/or speaker's words

- The recipients of the author and/or speaker's words

- How unique or specific the situation was to which the author and/or speaker addressed his words

- The significance of any differences between our situation and that of the original readers and/or hearers.

Let's look at an example of the use of these three questions in a matter relating to women in the church. Many have noted that Jesus appointed only men as apostles and have used this fact to justify limiting women's role in congregations in such areas as preaching, praying, baptizing, and leading. The point here is not to quibble with these interpretations, but to make it clear that they *are* interpretations, not what the text actually says. They seem to be based on the common assumption that the reason Jesus chose only men to be apostles was because it has always been God's intent that men lead and women follow. This would mean that Jesus was not at liberty to choose any women, if he was to be faithful to his Father's will. What this assumption fails to recognize is that the biblical text does not tell us *why* Jesus chose only men; it merely says *that* he did. In fact, the text does not make it a gender issue at all. Many other men and types of people, such as Gentiles or Samaritans, were not selected as well.

So when someone asserts that women are limited in what they may do in the church in part because Jesus did not appoint any women as apostles, they are not stating what the Bible says (first question), but rather their human interpretation of what it meant (second question). Let's not put too much weight on our opinion of Jesus' intent when the text does not give us any information on that.

This current book is essentially an exegetical study of relevant biblical passages dealing with women in the church, trying to ascertain what the author or speaker originally meant. As such it is concerned primarily with the first and second questions. However, exegesis is merely an academic exercise if it does not serve the purpose of hermeneutics or modern-day application. The third question will always be in the background and sometimes will be addressed directly.

Discussion Questions

1. How can we develop the habit of questioning our assumptions and viewing familiar passages with fresh eyes?

2. Can you think of an example of where it is important that we ask the first question, "What does it say?" before jumping to the second, "What did it mean?"

3. In your personal Bible study, why is it important to ask the modern-day application question, "What *does* it mean?" rather than simply being satisfied with the answer to "What *did* it mean?"

4. Can you think of a biblical passage where considering the context makes all the difference in understanding it correctly?

CHAPTER FOUR

The Creation Narrative

M ost Bible-based books and articles on the topic of women in the church begin with or at least concentrate on key NT passages in Paul's writings. Yet Paul's teachings are merely the end of a long biblical trajectory that goes all the way back to the creation. This current study will, therefore, begin with the creation story in Genesis 1-3, move to Jesus, and finally deal with Paul.

There are at least three reasons for beginning in Genesis. First, Jesus and Paul both draw on the creation account in Genesis in their comments on men and women. A correct understanding of what the Genesis text actually says and what it meant in its own context is an essential prerequisite to properly interpreting Jesus and Paul's references.

Second, among modern writers who do deal directly with the Genesis account of human origins, there is a great deal of disagreement on the interpretation of certain elements of the text and their relevance to the question of women in the church. Much of this disagreement centers on implications drawn from the text rather than what the text itself actually says or does not say.

Third, not a few studies on Genesis 1-3 introduce foreign terminology or concepts, such as "male spiritual leadership" or "designated spiritual protector," that are simply not found in the text. A careful examination of these chapters will quickly expose these inventions for what they are, so they can be disposed of when they reappear in NT discussions of women in the church.

Finally, in order to limit our study to what Genesis 1-3 says and meant in its own context, we must be careful not to introduce ideas that come from a later time, even NT times. Consequently, we will defer consideration of important NT references to the creation account to chapter five, where we can examine them in their own context. In the current chapter we are concerned with answering that second question (what did it mean?) to provide a proper foundation for considering the third (what does it mean?) later.

Examination of the Text

Prior to the Fall: Gen. 1:26-2:25

GENESIS 1 AND 2 PRESENT TWO COMPLEMENTARY ACCOUNTS of the creation of humankind. There is an essential unity between the two, but the perspective is different. Both use the word "humankind" or "man" (*'adam*), though differently. In Genesis 1 the word refers to both male and female, but in chapter 2 it designates a particular male individual. Further, both chapters discuss the origin of humankind as both male and female. Finally, each chapter presents male and female in relationship with each other, rather than as men and women in general.

First Account of Creation of Humans: Gen. 1:26-31. In this account both the male and the female comprise humankind (*'adam*) without any further distinctions. Both are created (*bara'*) in God's image and after His likeness without any additional details as to the method or order. Both are blessed (*bērak*) by God with the charge to populate the earth. Finally, both are given specific dominion over all the various elements of God's creation on earth. None of the many subsequent distinctions between men and women in specific situations or relationships come from this passage. Here they are merely male and female. Note further that this text has already introduced the idea of men and women interacting with each other as couples, as the instruction to "be fruitful and multiply" (1:28) suggests a sexual activity appropriately reserved to married partners.

Second Account of Creation of Humans: Gen. 2:4b-25

Exposition

WHAT WE NOW HAVE IS THE BEAUTIFUL STORY OF THE origin of the marriage relationship. Here it is presented as the answer to the human need for companionship (2:18, 20). This comes in response to the first time God concluded that something about his creation was *not* good. The man was alone. He needed a helper fit for him (2:18, 20). The man's own response was that here is a companion like him, yes even a part of him (2:23). This allowed them to share an intimacy completely without shame (2:25).

Verse 24 is not a part of the narrative, but rather the author's comment about its significance. Many have noted the oddity of applying this to a man leaving his family when he takes a wife, rather than a woman leaving hers, as was customary in the patriarchal society when this was written. William Grasham (2014, pp. 105-08) has argued plausibly that in a patriarchal society the wife had already left her family when she married. God's requirement here is that the husband must do the same. In ancient society a son's duty to his family was superseded only by his duty to God. God's intent in 2:24, however, is the shocking requirement that someone else, a man's wife, must now come before his parents. In this context, the force of the final words of verse 24 ("and they become one flesh") charges through. Here a relationship is created that is closer than that based on blood. What an exalted view of marriage!

From what the text of chapter two actually *says*, not what some have suggested it *implies*, two conclusions stand out. First, the entire focus of the chapter is on a husband and wife, not on men and women in general. Second, no hierarchy in the relationship of this married couple is in evidence. Pointing to the first is the fashioning of the woman to address an individual man's loneliness, the intimacy of the actual shaping of the woman from the one who was to be her husband, the man's delight at having his own companion, and the author's concluding application of all of this to future husbands and wives, including their sexual intimacy. The second conclusion has become more problematic in the interpretive history of this passage, not because of what the text actually says or does not say, but because of what certain interpreters say it implies. Because these opinions are so widely held, they will be noted and examined here.

Examination of Proposed Reasons for Interpreting Genesis 2 Hierarchically

THOSE WHO BELIEVE THAT FROM THE BEGINNING (BEFORE the fall) God intended man to be the leader generally support their convictions by implications they draw in one or more of the following areas: (1) *order* of creation, (2) *source* of creation, (3) *purpose* of creation, or (4) *naming* of the creatures.

Order of Creation. *It is argued that the man was created before the woman, which implies that he will be over her.* Were this the case, then the animals would be over man, but instead man was given dominion over all the animals (1:26).

You cannot have it both ways, that is, argue man's supremacy over the animals as the crowning and final act of creation while at the same time asserting the man's supremacy over the woman because he was created first. Note also the striking degree to which priority of appearance is no indication of ultimate status in the book of Genesis. Consider Cain, Abel and Seth; Isaac and Ishmael; Jacob and Esau; Rachel and Leah; Judah's sons; Ephraim and Manasseh; and Joseph and his brothers.

Source of Creation. *It is argued that the woman was fashioned from the man, which implies his position over her.* On the contrary, note that the man was formed from "dust of the ground" (2:7). Who would argue that the earth is somehow over the man? Certainly after the fall, the man's relationship with the ground will become problematic because it is cursed (3:17-19), but that was not the case from the beginning. Far from indicating the woman's subordination, the fact that she was made for companionship with her husband (2:18, 20) and came from his side (2:21) suggests that intimacy between the man and the woman is the real point, not status relative to each other.

Purpose of Creation. *It is argued that the fact that the woman was created to be the man's helper implies her subordination to him.* On the contrary, the Hebrew word translated "helper" (*'ezer*) (2:18, 20) is used 19 other places in the OT, 15 of which refer to God, including all the 11 occurrences in the Psalms. Typical is Ps. 121:1-2: "I lift up my eyes to the hills; where does my help come from? My help comes from the Lord, who made heaven and earth." Are we to conclude that God is to be subordinate to us because he is our helper? Rather, the author's point relates to companionship. God noted that something was missing—"it is not good that the man should be alone"—and he gave him someone "fit for him" in a way none of the animals could be (2:19-22). Again, intimacy, not status, is the point.

Naming of the Creatures. *It is argued that generally the leader names those under him, not the other way around. The man named the animals, over which he had dominion; so it was in giving the woman her name.* Aside from the fact that this interjects a notion into the text that is totally absent, what we have in 2:23 rather than a formal naming is a spontaneous expression of joy. Now at last here is someone like me ("bone of my bones and flesh of my flesh"). She is no less than my counterpart! This is indicated by the words for the two in the verse: "man" (*'ish*) and "woman" (*'ishshah*). The formal naming of his wife occurs after the fall (3:20).

Thus, to repeat the earlier-stated conclusion, (1) the entire focus of chapter 2 is on a husband and wife, not on men and women in general and (2) no hierarchy in the relationship of this married couple is in evidence.

The Fall and Aftermath: Gen. 3:1-24

GEN. 3:16, WHERE THE WRITER LISTS THE THREEFOLD consequence of Eve's sin, has become ground zero in the conflict over the impact of the Genesis creation account on the matter of women in the church. The verse has been so picked apart that one wonders if there is anything that can be said about it for certain. Here are some of the questions that have emerged in the discussion: (1) whether it reflects a curse or punishment or consequence or natural result of sin, (2) whether the source of the consequences is God Himself or the natural result of their sin, (3) the interconnection among the three elements of the verse, (4) the meaning of "desire," and (5) the meaning of "rule." All these will be considered in due course, but first it is important to address what the text actually says about the fall and its multiple consequences.

Exposition

Temptation and Disobedience (3:1-7). The serpent's temptation of the woman involved the trickery ("the serpent was more crafty," 3:1) of changing God's command by only one word (from "you will surely die" to "you will *not* surely die") and adding the enticement of becoming like God by obtaining knowledge that only He had (3:1-5). Of the three characteristics of the fruit that drew her, it was "that it was to be desired to make one wise" that was the real temptation (3:6). Beauty and desirability for food were features of all the fruit trees in the garden (2:9). The writer ascribes none of this temptation to her husband. The text simply says that she gave him some of the fruit and he ate it. This experience of disobedience brought to them a knowledge they had not had before—that they were naked (3:7), unlike their previous state (2:25).

Confrontation by God (3:8-13). After his sin, the prospect of a further encounter with God also brought the man something he had not experienced before—fear (3:10), and it caused them to hide. At this point the blame game begins. The man tries to deflect the culpability from himself to his companion and by extension to God Himself (3:12). Now for the first time the woman has a solo direct encounter with God, and she tries to blame that crafty creature (3:1), the serpent, for deceiving her.

The Consequences (3:14-19). Three general points deserve attention before looking at how God responded to each party: (1) curse or no curse,? (2) one or more punishments for each party,? and (3) "because you have."

Curse or No Curse? One of the first things a careful reading of the text reveals is that there are only two curses in Genesis 3, and neither of them is on the woman or the man. Only the serpent (3:14) and the ground (3:17) are cursed (*'arar*), although the curse on the ground is for the man's sake. This is in stark contrast with much of the literature on this passage, where the word "curse" is thrown around in places where the writer never put it, especially with reference to the man and the woman. So what do we call what happened to this couple as a result of their sin? "Consequence" probably has the least baggage associated with it and is widely used in the literature. "Punishment" is also faithful to the text, because it is God's response to their sin. To the woman God said, "I will greatly multiply your pain in childbearing. . . ." (3:16) and to the man, "because you have. . ., cursed is the ground for your sake. . ." (3:17-19).

One or More Than One Punishment for Each Party? This issue has to do with whether the different elements of the consequences of the sin for each party are tied together or are independent punishments. Although either is possible, at least in the case of 3:16, the three elements make better sense taken together than they do as independent consequences. Given the intensity of pain and perhaps even the great danger of death in childbirth, a wife might forego sexual intimacy with her husband, even to the point of disrupting God's original intent that humankind "be fruitful and multiply and fill the earth" (1:28). Her desire for her husband will override that instinct, but it will also include rulership over her by the one for whom she has the desire.

"Because You Have." In the case of the serpent and the man, God confronted them with the accusation, "because you have" (3:14, 17), but He did not with the woman. With the serpent His grievance was no more specific than "because you have done this" (3:14). With the man, however, God identified two aspects of his disobedience, one the actual disobedience ("you have eaten of the tree of which I commanded you, 'you shall not eat of it'") and the other what led to it ("you have listened to the voice of your wife") (3:17). The fact that God did not specify the woman's sin has opened the door to speculation that goes beyond anything the author actually wrote, so we should be content with that and move on.

Consequences for the Serpent (3:14-15). The serpent's punishment contained the element of a curse. Henceforth he would go on his belly, eating dust (3:14). The bruising of his head (3:15) may simply be the consequence of the serpent's position on the ground, but a popular alternative Christian interpretation is that the bruising will be done by the Messiah. This view goes beyond what the Genesis text actually says, answering the later question, what does it mean?, so it is beyond the scope of our current exegesis of the text in its own context.

Consequences for the Man (3:17-19). As noted above, the man is not cursed directly, but the ground is cursed because of him. This is his punishment, and the vocation God had earlier given him to till the ground (2:5) or till and keep the garden (2:15) would now involve labor (the same Hebrew word used of the woman in 3:16) and sweat because of the thorns and thistles the ground would bring forth.

Consequences for the Woman (3:16).

3:16a. At least this part of the punishment is prescribed by God Himself ("I will greatly multiply your pain. . . ."). The consequence of the woman's sin is more *pain* in childbearing, not the childbearing itself, because that was already a part of

God's plan, as He indicated in His blessing to "be fruitful and multiply" (1:28). The word for "pain" (*'issabon*) is the same one translated "labor" in the judgment on the man in 3:17, an apt descriptor for the birthing experience.

3:16b. The key issue in this part of the verse is the meaning of "desire" (*t³šuqah*), a word used elsewhere in the OT only in Gen. 4:7 and Song of Sol. 7:11(10). Though some find Gen. 4:7 as the closer parallel for deciding the word's meaning in 3:16b, its use in the Song of Solomon of a bridegroom's desire for his bride comes much closer to the context of 3:16b. Hence, the most reasonable interpretation of the nuance of "desire" in 3:16b is the woman's sexual desire for her husband.

3:16c. The interpretive history of these words, "and he will rule over you," has had such an enormous impact on discussions of women in the church that a simple exegesis in the context (i.e., asking the questions what does it say? and what did it mean?) does not exhaust the possibilities. However, since this chapter on the creation narrative is limiting itself to those two questions, we will defer other related matters to the next chapter on how Genesis 1-3 is used in the NT. Any new information learned there can then be added to what our exegetical study here has concluded.

The key issue in 3:16c is the meaning of "rule" (*masal*). By far the majority of interpreters follow this meaning of the word, but a small number of them define *masal* as "*harsh* rule," not simple "rule." It is rule that might even be described as spousal abuse. Thus, the consequence for the woman would not simply be her husband's rule of her, but a rule characterized by force or dominance. However, the Hebrew verb in the OT has a wide range of meanings, some of which are even the opposite of harshness. In fact, in Isa. 40:10 and 63:19 *masal* refers to God's benevolent rule over his people. Thus, in Gen. 3:16c, God is simply telling the woman that her husband will rule over her, without further characterizing the nature of that rule.

Conclusions

GENESIS 1-3 TELLS THE STORY OF PARADISE GAINED AND paradise lost for the first married couple. The narrative moves from joint vocation without gender distinction (chapter one) to companionship in paradise (chapter two) to the ugly effects of sin as that companionship is damaged and the gender distinction enters the relationship (chapter three). The text does offer a brief glimpse of the impact of the story on future humankind ("have dominion over. . ."—1:26, 28; "fill the earth and subdue it"—1:28; "therefore a man leaves his father and his mother. . ."—2:24). However, the story as it stands in Gen. 1-3 is one of a specific married couple and the effect on *them*. Subsequent biblical writers will return to this narrative and draw conclusions about its impact on future persons (answering the question, what *does* it mean?), but the writer of these chapters in Genesis does not, with the exception of the verses noted above. What is abundantly clear is that the entire narrative refers to a married couple, not to men and women in general.

Discussion Questions

1. Why do you think the author began this study of women in the church with Genesis 1-3 rather than passages in the New Testament?

2. What evidence is there in Genesis 1-3 that the creation narrative is or is not primarily about a husband and wife, rather than men and women generically?

3. Were the man and the woman in the creation narrative in a hierarchal relationship prior to the Fall (Genesis 3)? Support your answer from the text.

4. What word do you think best describes what happened to the man and woman as a result of their sin—punishment, curse, consequence, or some other word?

CHAPTER FIVE

New Testament Use of the Genesis Creation Narrative

Chapter four attempted to answer the questions "what does it say?" and "what did it mean?" in the Genesis creation narrative by interpreting it in its own context. This, of course, begs the question, "what *does* it mean?," as we consider the contribution of the rest of the Bible, especially the NT, toward gaining a fuller picture of how these three chapters should be understood. Much of the use of the OT by NT writers and speakers interprets OT texts in a literal, straightforward manner. However, a number of passages use interpretive methods that draw meanings that cannot be derived solely from the OT text itself. All of this flows from an underlying belief that in addition to the literal sense, for many OT passages God intended a secondary meaning. Words like "deeper," "spiritual," "allegorical," or "mystery" are commonly used to describe this meaning behind or below the literal one. In this chapter we will look at how NT writers and speakers used and interpreted the Genesis creation narrative in passages that are relevant to the matter of women in the church.

Types of References

THERE ARE 37 CLEAR AND POSSIBLE REFERENCES TO GENESIS 1-3 found in 14 NT books. This chapter will probe the use of the Genesis creation narrative in these passages, which means that the discussion will be limited to Jesus and Paul. These 37 references are discussed below according to their type, either (1) direct quotations, (2) verbal allusions (where actual words from an OT passage appear, though not in a direct quotation), or (3) non-verbal allusions (where an OT passage is alluded to without any of its actual words being used).

Jewish Interpretive Methods During the New Testament Period

IN ORDER TO APPRECIATE THE MULTIPLE WAYS IN WHICH NT speakers and writers use the OT, we need to look briefly at three approaches used by first-century Jews to derive secondary or fuller meanings from OT passages that go beyond the literal interpretation. These are (1) Midrashic, (2) Allegorical, and (3) *Rāz-Pesher*. Paul is an example of one NT author who used all three.

Midrashic

THIS APPROACH WAS USED BY THE RABBINIC JUDAISM (THE Pharisees) of Jesus and Paul's day. It was the way Paul, as a star rabbinical student of the leading rabbi of his day (Acts 22:3), was trained to interpret the OT. Jesus would have seen this method used every week at his synagogue. The midrashic approach draws inferences from various elements of single or multiple passages, usually without regard for the context. For example, if a certain word is used in one verse, it is inferred that it had a similar meaning in another. What is noteworthy about the way NT authors and speakers use similar interpretive principles is the comparative restraint and reasonableness of their conclusions when set alongside those of contemporary rabbinic Judaism.

Allegorical

IN THIS CONTEXT, AN ALLEGORY IS AN ADDITIONAL OR deeper meaning that is not obvious from a literal reading of the text. This method is most closely associated with Greek-speaking Alexandrians, where at least as early as the middle of the second century BC Jews were allegorizing the OT. The philosopher-theologian most associated with the method was Philo. While Philo did not deny the validity of the literal meaning of an OT passage, he used his Greek learning to derive additional or deeper meanings.

The Gospels contain no examples of Jesus' use of allegory to interpret the OT, but Jesus did provide allegorical interpretations of some of his parables. In dealing with the OT, however, he found himself referred to in the Scriptures in ways that were not obvious to the uninstructed reader (Luke 24:27, 44-47). So, even though Jesus may not have employed allegory in his OT interpretation in the usual manner of the day, these interpretations went beyond the literal to the underlying meaning of the text. Paul identifies his method of interpreting the story of Hagar and Sarah as allegory (Gal. 4:24), and his writings contain three other clear allegorical interpretations of the OT (I Cor. 5:6-8, 9:8-10, and 10:1-11).

Rāz-Pesher (Mystery-Interpretation)

ONE OF THE FEATURES THAT DISTINGUISHED NT SPEAKers and writers from the rabbis and the Alexandrian allegorists in their interpretation of the OT is their seeing themselves as living in the end times foreseen in OT prophesies. The same can be said about the community that produced the Dead Sea Scrolls. Here we find theological treatises and biblical commentaries written by a community that believed *they* were living in the end times and were the specific intended subject of OT prophesies. It appears that the early church and the Qumran community had a common source for this type of OT interpretation—the Book of Daniel.

In the dream interpretation narratives in Daniel, God's message came in two stages. God communicated both the dream/vision and the interpretation. Without the interpretation (*pesher*), the dream remained a mystery (*rāz*). The Greek word *musterion* (mystery) always translates the Aramaic word *rāz* in the Book of Daniel, where it is always used of a mystery concealed in a dream. In Paul's use of the Greek word *musterion*, he, like the Qumran community, affirmed that the second act of revelation, the interpretation, identified his own day as the time of fulfillment (see, e.g., Rom. 16:25b-26, Eph. 1:9-10, and 3:3-11).

Whereas the rabbis controlled their OT exegesis by adherence to certain rules or principles of interpretation, and Philo thought that only through much learning and experience could one interpret the OT at the deeper level, God inspired the Christian apostles and prophets (Eph. 3:5) to explain how it points to the time in which they were living. No longer does a veil obscure the end-time message of the OT, because "through Christ it is taken away" (II Cor. 3:14-16). Herein lies the uniqueness of the use of the OT in the NT.

Jesus and Paul's Use of the Old Testament in Passages Relevant to This Study

Direct Quotations

Matthew 19:4-5=Mark 10:6-8a. In both Matthew and Mark's version of Jesus' encounter with the Pharisees over divorce, Jesus connects a few words from Gen. 1:27 with a full quotation of Gen. 2:24. In Matthew he ascribes the words to God Himself ("the Creator"). In the words, "therefore what God has joined together, let man not separate," Jesus relates 2:24 to future married couples. Significantly, then, Jesus applies these two verses to individual men and women in a marriage relationship with each other, not to men and women in general.

Ephesians 5:31. Paul also quotes Gen. 2:24, but his use and interpretation of the verse could not be more different than that of Jesus. Whereas Jesus took the passage in a straightforward, literal way to support his opposition to divorce, Paul put forward an underlying interpretation in the manner of allegory. Because of his identification of the verse as a mystery (*mustērion*), Eph. 5:32 has the earmarks of a *rāz-pesher* interpretation. At the literal level, the verse has to do with the marriage of a man and a woman, but there is a mystery in those literal words pointing to a deeper meaning much more sublime than human marriage—that of Christ and the church. In the way Paul uses Gen. 2:24, he highlights the exceptionally high value God places on this human relationship. It makes all the more understandable Paul's opposition to Christians getting a divorce (I Cor. 7:10-13, 27, 39) and links up with Jesus' own opposition to this action when he interpreted Gen. 2:24.

Clear Verbal and Non-verbal Allusions

Galatians 3:28. The words "male and female" (*arsen kai thēlu*) in 3:28 appear to be a verbal allusion to Gen. 1:27. This is suggested by the fact that their structure breaks with the pattern in the other two pairs and reproduces the wording of the Septuagint in Gen. 1:27. "Jew *nor* (*oude*) Greek," "slave *nor* (*oude*) free" becomes "male *and* (*kai*) female" in the final pair. Although many have speculated on what Paul's reason was for choosing this wording here, Paul himself does not tell us, so we should just leave it at that.

I Corinthians 11:8, 9. Verses 8 and 9 are clear allusions to Gen. 2:22-23 and 2:18, 20 respectively. Here Paul interprets these texts in a literal, straightforward way to support his statement at the end of verse 7 that "the wife is the glory of the husband." As was shown in the discussion of Genesis 2 in chapter four, everything in Genesis 2 has to do with a husband and wife, not men and women in general. Hence, any interpretation of Paul's use of Genesis 2 here that takes his reference in a straightforward way necessarily connects these as instructions to husbands and wives, not men and women in the church.

II Corinthians 11:3. Here Paul makes a non-verbal allusion to the serpent's temptation of Eve in Gen. 3:4-5 and a verbal allusion to Eve's response to God in Gen. 3:13, "the serpent deceived me." He does not use the reference to Genesis 3 to prove a point, as he does in references to OT texts in several other places, but rather to draw an analogy from Eve's deception by the serpent to the Corinthian church's risk of being deceived by the false apostles (11:13). Paul interprets the Genesis narrative here in a literal, straightforward way.

I Timothy 2:13, 14. I Tim. 2:13-14 has become ground zero in the dispute over the traditional versus a wider role for women in the church. While 2:12 has probably had a greater impact on limiting what women may do in the church than any other passage in the Bible, verses 13-14 have been employed as the coup de grace in the defense of the traditional view. Thus the question of how Paul uses the OT in these two verses is critical to the present study.

Verse 13 makes a verbal allusion to Gen. 2:7-8, 15 (*plassō, to form*) and a non-verbal allusion to the fashioning of Eve from a part of Adam in Gen. 2:21-22. Verse 14 is a verbal allusion to Gen. 3:13, where the woman made the excuse that the serpent had *deceived* her (*apataō, to deceive*). In considering Paul's point in these allusions to the creation narrative, many interpreters have observed correctly that he does not tell us what it is. He merely makes the allusions and connects them back to 2:11-12 by the word "for" (*gar*) in 2:13.

2:13. The traditional interpretation of 2:13 is that Paul is making a point of primogeniture, the higher status of the one who is prior in time. While that is possible, its normal application in the OT, where it appears frequently, is to the birth order of brothers. More probable, in light of the original context in Genesis 2, is that Paul is alluding to the *companionship* of this first married couple brought about by the way they were brought together. Seen this way, Paul is making an historical allusion to the creation account that shows that he is talking primarily about *married* women, i.e., women who are in a relationship like Adam and Eve's. *First* Adam was alone, and *then* the Lord God fashioned Eve and brought her to him to make them a married couple. In the context of I Timothy, where marriage was under attack (4:3), this would make perfect sense.

2:14. Just as with 2:13, Paul does not tell us what his point is in verse 14. Until recently the rather uniform understanding of Paul's meaning has been that he is arguing that woman's ability to resist temptation is weaker than man's. Thus she should not be allowed to teach or be in a position of authority over men (2:12). There are a number of problems with this interpretation, not the least of which is that Paul himself does not make that application here, nor does the creation narrative to which Paul is referring even hint at such an inherent weakness in Eve. In fact, if Eve's deception is the theological basis of women in Ephesus not teaching men, how is it that Paul was not similarly disqualified? In Rom. 7:11 he acknowledges that he himself sinned having been deceived, and here he uses exactly the same verb for deception (*exapataō*) that he uses of Eve in I Tim. 2:14 and II Cor. 11:3.

Some recent interpreters, while rejecting the notion of women's greater susceptibility to temptation, still cling to the view that Paul is using this reference to the creation narrative to disqualify women from teaching men (2:12). They usually suggest one of two alternative interpretations, either that (1) Eve was the first to transgress or that (2) Eve was guilty of role reversal. In connection with the first, although we know from Gen. 3:6 that Eve ate the fruit first, I Tim. 2:14 says nothing about that. 2:14 talks about the woman's deception in contrast with Adam, not who transgressed first. Inexplicably, here a key interpretation of 2:11-12 is based on something that 2:14 does not even say. The second alternative interpretation, role reversal, assumes that Eve was already in a subordinate position to her husband at the time she ate the fruit, a notion that is not borne out either by the text in the Genesis narrative or by Paul's use of it. Neither Genesis nor Paul indicate that Eve's sin was not being submissive to her husband by leading him.

What, then, is Paul's point in contrasting the woman's deception with Adam's lack of it? An attempt to reconstruct the situation in Ephesus to which I Timothy was written holds the best promise for finding a reasonable answer. Whatever that background was for I Tim. 2:8-15, it seems clear that as far as what was going on in the Ephesian assemblies is concerned, the problem centered on the women (seven verses) more than the men (one verse). Chapter eleven of this book discusses whether the problem lay with the content of these women's teaching or the manner, concluding that it was likely the latter. That discussion presents evidence that these women (actually wives) were teaching in a domineering way, which was not consistent with the proper submissiveness of women to their husbands, particularly in public. This was disruptive to the tranquility Christians are to pray for in their lives (2:2) and that should characterize their assemblies.

So what does Paul's allusions to the creation narrative in 2:13-14 have to do with his limitation on women's behavior in 2:11-12? The original purpose of woman was to be a companion to her husband (Gen. 2:18, 20). To this end, Adam having been formed first, Eve was formed next to be with him. This is where 2:13 fits. However, "trouble in Paradise" came when through deception the woman became a transgressor (Gen. 3:6, 13; I Tim. 2:14). This now becomes analogous to the situation with wives in the assemblies in Ephesus. So here Paul uses an analogy or cautionary biblical illustration to support his restriction on these wives' teaching, much like he does in I Cor. 10:7-10 and II Cor. 11:3.

One final, critical point remains. The allusions to the Genesis creation narrative in I Tim. 2:13-15 demonstrates that Paul is not discussing Christian women in general in 2:13-14, but Christian wives. The woman was formed for a particular man, her husband (2:13). The woman sinned when she was deceived by the serpent in the presence of her husband (2:14). Among the consequences of the woman's sin was increased pain in childbirth (2:15), a result coming from an intimate activity between a particular man and woman. There is no justification for applying the Genesis creation narrative generally or the three references to it in I Tim. 2:13-15 to women in general in Ephesus.

I Timothy 2:15. Whether this is a possible or probable verbal allusion to Gen. 3:16 is an open question. The verbal similarity is clearly there. The word for "childbearing" in I Tim. 2:15 is *teknogonia*. In Gen. 3:16 the phrase "she will bear children" is rendered in the Septuagint by two words, the verb *tiktō* and the noun *teknon*. It is not a perfect verbal match, but the meaning is the same, thereby rendering it a probable verbal allusion. To what "childbearing" refers, however, is one of the most disputed points in the entire epistle.

Possible Verbal Allusions

I Corinthians 11:7. The question here is whether 11:7b ("being the image and glory of God") is an allusion to the Genesis creation narrative or not. If it is, how do we explain it? Two factors point away from identifying the reference with Gen. 1:26-27: (1) although the word "image" (*eikōn*) is found in the Genesis narrative (1:26, 27, 5:1), the word "glory" (*doxa*) is not and (2) the female is also in the image of God (1:27). So, while it is possible that 11:7b is a reference to Genesis 1, these two considerations make it unlikely.

I Corinthians 11:3, 14:34, and I Timothy 2:12. As noted above, there is a probable verbal allusion to Gen. 3:16a in the word "childbearing" (*teknogonia*) in I Tim. 2:15. The question here is whether Paul is alluding to Gen. 3:16c, "he will rule over you," in any of these three verses. Many interpreters on both sides of the matter of women in the church assume that Gen.3:16c is at least part of the basis of Paul's teaching on the relationship of husbands and wives in particular, if not men and women in general in the church. Yet there is no verbal connection between these verses and Gen. 3:16c. This makes the assumed link mere conjecture, without supporting evidence. In fact, spreading the net wider, no other passage in the NT points to Gen. 3:16c. Therefore, the most reasonable conclusion is to question the widely held view that Gen. 3:16c is in the background in these verses.

But what about the OT? There is a complete absence of references to the consequences of Adam and Eve's sin after the Genesis creation narrative in the rest of the OT. Adam is mentioned in only two other places later in the OT, and Eve is never mentioned again. Further, although there are voluminous examples in the OT of patriarchy being the norm in the family and in society at large, nowhere does the OT connect this with God's intent in the creation, much less with Gen. 3:16. Thus, other than a possible allusion to Gen. 3:16a in I Tim. 2:15, there is no clear reference to Gen. 3:16 in either the OT or the NT.

Conclusions

THIS EXAMINATION OF THE NT USE OF THE GENESIS creation narrative has confirmed two points made in the discussion of the creation narrative in chapter four of this book. First, the Genesis creation narrative relates only to a husband and his wife. No allusions to Genesis 1-3 in the NT relate to men and women in general in the church. In fact, there is no clear passage in the entire Bible that puts women in general under men in general. Second, Jesus applies even Gen. 1:27 to married couples, not to men and women generally.

At two points the NT provides new information about Genesis 1-3. First, Paul's *rāz-pesher* interpretation of Gen. 2:24 in Eph. 5:31-32 as referring to the spiritual union of Christ and the church adds a meaning to Gen. 2:24 that an exegesis of that verse could never have produced. Second, Paul's use of Gen. 2:22-23 and 2:18, 20 to support his assertion that "the wife is the glory of the husband" (I Cor. 11:7) gives new information about those verses.

Discussion Questions

1. Explain some of the methods Jews at the time of Jesus and Paul used to interpret the Old Testament.

2. Compare and contrast Jesus and Paul's use of Gen. 2:24 to show the high value God places on human marriage.

3. What evidence is there, if any, that "he will rule over you" from Gen. 3:16c is the basis of any New Testament teaching about the relationship between men and women in either the church or the family?

4. How does the New Testament use of verses from Genesis 1-3 help our understanding of the roles of men and women in marriage and in the church?

CHAPTER SIX

Women in the World of Jesus

Jesus was born into a world that, for women, was different from our Western world in almost every way imaginable. Jewish women in Palestine and other places in the East were greatly limited in the circles in which they operated. The norm was to get married after they reached majority at age 12½. Except for religious observances, like going to the Synagogue or Temple, their activities were almost entirely at home or in support of their duties there. The wife's purpose was to bear and bring up children, thereby enabling her husband to fulfil his obligation to obey God's command to "be fruitful and multiply" (Gen. 1:28). She had little contact with men other than those in her household, and when she went out she was veiled. Men engaged in the public activities, and although women participated in festivals, they were excluded from some of the ceremonial obligations prescribed in the Law of Moses. Although the provision for a "bill of divorce" (Deut. 24:1-4) gave wives some protection from insensitive husbands who wanted to get rid of them, in actual practice they could be divorced on almost any pretext. While at home, a minor daughter remained under the care and protection—and watchful eye—of her father. That state was merely transferred to her husband when she married. Such is the picture drawn in the Mishnah, our best source for Pharisaic Judaism in Palestine at the time of Jesus.

So, what signals did Jesus send that the situation for women who would become his disciples would change or be about the same? What would his followers learn from his words and his actions that would signify the direction they should go in these matters? Those questions will be addressed in the next chapter. As background for that discussion, this chapter will survey the state of women in first-century Palestine, particularly as reflected in the Mishnah.

Women in First-Century Palestine

So what is the Mishnah? It is a collection of sayings of the Palestinian rabbis from approximately the late first century BC through the second century AD. No other source gives us in one place better insight into the world of the Pharisees with whom Jesus sparred on numerous occasions. In the evidence from the Mishnah that follows, we get the flavor of how the Torah was being applied in Palestine in Jesus' day on matters relating to women.

The Mishnah contains 63 tractates or chapters, divided into six divisions. The third division is called "Women" and contains the following seven tractates: "Sisters-in-law," "Marriage Deeds," "Vows," "The Nazirite Vow," "The Suspected Adulteress," "Bills of Divorce," and "Betrothals." "The Menstruant" in the sixth division also deals with women's matters, as do individual passages in many other tractates. What follows is a survey of some of the key teachings of the Mishnah and two other first-century AD sources on eight topics related to women.

Social Status

Women were commonly grouped with slaves and children in the Mishnah. In one passage at least, they were even ranked lower than Samaritans.

Submission

NUMEROUS PASSAGES DEAL WITH THE INTRICACIES OF A WOMan's submission to her father or husband in her home. In general, a woman was under the control of her father until she reached majority at age 12 ½ or became married. If she was still a minor, her father had control over her betrothal. Further, if she was a minor when betrothed she was under the control of both her father and future husband until she reached majority. If she found something, it belonged to her father, as did her earnings if she worked. The father could even nullify his minor daughter's vows. What is abundantly clear from the multitude of passages about a woman's subordination to her father and husband is the absence of opinions placing women in general under the control of men in general. Just as in the OT, in the Judaism of the time of Jesus reflected in the Mishnah, the subordination of women as women applied only within the family.

Property

WHEN A MAN MARRIED A WIFE, HE WAS SEEN AS GETTING possession of her. This, of course, is not the same as saying that a wife was the property of her husband, as some have suggested. It is worthy of note, however, that in one passage the acquisition of a wife is discussed in the context of acquiring slaves, cattle, and physical property.

A man may make a prenuptial agreement allowing his wife to have full or partial control over her property, and it is valid. If she dies first, he inherits her property. But if she acquires property after she is married, it belongs to her husband. In this case, she is in the same position as a minor son or daughter or a foreign slave but in a lower position than a son or daughter of age or a Hebrew slave.

During her lifetime the husband also has the use of his wife's inheritance.

A special category dealing with property has to do with family inheritance rights. If a woman inherits something before she is betrothed, she may give it away or sell it. If, however, a woman disposes of inherited property after she is married, the husband may nullify the deal. The Mishnah is also quite specific about the inheritance or lack of it for daughters. First of all, while a father had wide ranging authority over his minor unmarried daughter, that did not extend to the use of her inherited property. Further, following Num. 27:8, if a man died without a son, his daughter received the inheritance, and she passed it on to her offspring. Thus she and her offspring's rights precede those of her father's brothers. However, if there is a son, he gets the inheritance, not the daughter. So how did an unmarried daughter survive after the death of her father? In the case where the inheritance was substantial, the sons provided for their sister's maintenance. If, however, it was small, she, rather than the sons, got the inheritance. What may seem unusual preferential treatment for the daughter actually makes perfect sense, given the greater ability of a man to support himself in that culture than a woman.

Teaching Children

NEITHER AN UNMARRIED MAN NOR A WOMAN WAS allowed to be a teacher of children.

Social Contact outside the Family

THE RABBIS WERE CONCERNED ABOUT CONTACT BETWEEN men and women. A man could not remain alone with two women (unless his wife was present), but a woman could remain alone with two men. Restrictions on contact between the sexes applied to public activities as well. Thus, it was considered a breach of Jewish custom if a woman spins in the street or speaks with a man outside the home. If a woman did not show proof of her virginity on her marriage bed and she had been seen talking with an unidentified man in the street, R. Joshua said this alone is enough to presume that she had had intercourse with him. So strict were the customs that if a man was alone with his betrothed in her father's house, it could not be assumed that they did not have intercourse.

Lest the impression be left that women were secluded in their homes, a number of activities outside the home are mentioned in the Mishnah. Among these are drawing water from a spring; working in the harvest or picking olives; operating as a shopkeeper; winnowing, grinding, or sifting corn with a neighbor woman; going to a house of mourning or a wedding feast; and celebrating in festivals in Jerusalem. There was also a Court of Women in the Temple with an upper gallery for women to observe men below without interacting with them.

Marriage

ACCORDING TO JOSEPHUS, THE FIRST-CENTURY PALESTINian Jewish historian, men were to be honorable in acquiring a wife from one who was authorized to give her away. Because woman was inferior to man in every respect, she was to be submissive that she might be directed by the man, to whom God had given all authority. However, this submission should not be used to humiliate her.

When a man was betrothed to a woman, it was assumed that she would be a virgin on her wedding night. If on the wedding night he learns that she is not a virgin, he can go to court for damages. If a girl who is still a minor is seduced, her father (not the girl herself) is due compensation. If her father dies before the fine is paid, her brothers' rights to the money precede her own, presumably because the brothers assume their deceased father's responsibility for her maintenance.

Although a woman taken as a captive in war was at the mercy of the man who wanted her as his wife, Josephus indicates that special protections were, nonetheless, provided for her. Scattered throughout the Mishnah are a number of other protections for a wife, such as where a husband may move with his wife without her consent. However, in the Mishnah the rights are heavily weighted in favor of the husband. For example, the wife was required to perform certain duties for her husband, including cooking, baking, grinding flour, clothes washing, nursing children, wool working, and making her husband's bed.

Divorce

WOMEN WERE NOT ALLOWED TO DIVORCE THEIR HUSBANDS, but in certain extreme cases they could insist that their husbands divorce them. The courts would also require that a man put his wife away if he abandoned her or denied her her conjugal rights for a specified period. According to Philo, the first-century Alexandrian Jewish author, if a husband is proven to have made a false charge of premarital unchastity against his new wife, he is fined and subjected to corporal punishment and must remain with her if she will have him. But if she wants to leave the marriage, she may do so, and he cannot stop her.

While the School of Shammai took the phrase, "some indecency," in Deut. 24:1 to allow a man to put away his wife only for sexual impropriety, the School of Hillel broadened the pretexts for divorce to almost anything, including spoiling a dish, the wife's becoming a deaf-mute, the wife's barrenness, or if he finds someone else more beautiful. Both

Josephus and Philo also show their familiarity with the widespread practice of their day of men putting away their wives for many causes. Total control was in the man's hands, because he did not need his wife's consent to put her away.

When a couple married, the husband pledged a *ketubah* to his wife. It is a specified amount of money she will be paid if he divorces her or dies. This had the effect of making it difficult for a man to divorce his wife, if he had trouble raising the money. However, there was a catch. If the wife transgressed the Law of Moses or certain Jewish customs he could put her away without paying the *ketubah*. Also, under certain circumstances, if certain defects were found in the woman, her betrothal could be invalidated or if married she could be put away without her *ketubah*.

Women's Testimony

HERE THE EVIDENCE IS MIXED. JOSEPHUS CLASSES WOMEN with slaves as those whose testimony was not accepted in court. According to a statement in the Mishnah, presumably women were not allowed to be judges or witnesses in cases involving property. On the other hand, the Mishnah discusses cases where a woman's testimony was heard, although it might be limited in certain instances. On the matter of making a guilt offering for refusing to testify on something that has been witnessed (Lev. 5:1, 5-6), women were exempt, but the passage does not explicitly forbid their testimony.

Conclusions

THE RELIGIOUS LEADERS WITH WHOM JESUS SPARRED throughout his ministry had developed a set of traditional applications of the Law of Moses that went well beyond the

Law itself. To these men it was "a hedge around the Torah" that enabled them to avoid transgressing God's laws. To Jesus it was oppressive and hypocritical legalism that was a burden to the common people (Matt. 23:4, 13; Luke 11:46, 52) and actually *caused* them to transgress God's laws (Matt. 15:3-6, 23:23; Mark 7:8-13; Luke 11:42). The Mishnah preserves the male-centered world view of "the scribes and Pharisees." These views were in continuity with certain elements of the Torah, such as the gender of the priests and the requirement for all males to perform certain religious obligations (Ex. 23:17=Deut. 16:16). However, as Jesus pointed out, at least in the case of God's protection for married women, the Pharisees were out of step with the intent or spirit of the Torah (Matt. 19:4-9=Mark 10:5-9).

This issue of divorce itself highlights the difference between Jesus' approach and that of his religious antagonists. While Jesus taught that God's original intent was that men should not divorce their wives at all (Matt. 19:8, Mark 10:9), the Mishnah contains a whole tractate dedicated to the intricacies of how the protection for women provided by Deut. 24:1-4 should be applied in everyday situations ("Bills of Divorce"). This tractate illustrates a characteristic of the entire Mishnah, namely that it is written to aid males in the performance of their religious duties. According to Lev. 15:24, a man could become ceremonially unclean by having sex with his wife while she was menstruating, so a whole tractate of the Mishnah is dedicated to bodily discharges, especially blood during menstruation ("The Menstruant"). So if a wife had sex with her husband during this period of uncleanness, he could put her away without her *ketubah*. A man could violate the law by eating food that had not been prepared properly or had not been tithed, so his wife could be put away, again without her *ketubah*, if she served him such food. And the list goes on and on. Jesus' attitude toward women was very different and more in line with positive examples of women found in the OT and intertestamental literature. With this background in place, we will now turn in the next chapter to Jesus' counter-cultural stance on women as pictured in the Gospels.

Discussion Questions

1. Picture yourself as an eleven-year-old girl in first-century Palestine. What expectations would you likely have about what your life would look like by the time you were twenty?

2. Do you think women in the Old Testament had less or greater freedom than their sisters in first-century Palestine? If you see a difference, how do you account for it?

3. According to the Pharisees, what responsibilities did husbands and wives have toward each other in Palestine in Jesus' day?

4. What protections did Jewish women in Palestine in Jesus' day have in their marriages? Where were they most vulnerable?

CHAPTER SEVEN

Jesus and Women

Having laid the groundwork in the preceding chapter for understanding the position of women in Palestine in Jesus' day, we are now ready to examine his refreshingly revolutionary stance on women. We probably should not consider Jesus' attitude and actions toward women apart from his counter-cultural stance on other marginalized groups. When it came to treating everyone with dignity without regard to his/her social standing, Jesus was inflexibly compassionate and evenhanded. Thus, it should not surprise us to find Jesus acting toward women the same way he treated other disenfranchised people. This chapter is an examination of how women appear in Jesus' teachings, his teachings about women, and finally, his association with women.

Women in Jesus' Teachings

HERE HE IS NOT MUCH DIFFERENT THAN THE RABBIS. BOTH he and they used women sparingly in stories or parables to illustrate points. In Jesus' case, women appear in four parables: (1) the parable of the woman who hid leaven in meal (Matt. 13:33=Luke 13:20-21), (2) the parable of the ten maidens (Matt. 25:1-13), (3) the parable of the lost coins (Luke 15:8-10), and (4) the parable of the unjust judge (Luke 18:1-8). They also appear in an illustration about a woman in labor (John 16:21) and in a prediction in the Synoptic Apocalypse about two women grinding at the mill (Matt. 24:41=Luke 17:35). Finally, in his dispute with the scribes and Pharisees over their seeking a sign, he made an OT reference to the queen of the South in his critique of them (Matt. 12:42=Luke 11:31). Where Jesus is markedly different from the Palestinian rabbis, however, is in the other two areas, namely, in his teachings *about* women and in his association *with* them.

Jesus' Teachings about Women

THE GOSPELS RECORD NO SAYINGS WHERE JESUS DISCUSSES the topic of women as a class, so there is nothing from which we can construct a theology of women according to Jesus. There are three highly significant areas, though, where women appear in his teachings: (1) occasions when he paid a woman a high compliment, (2) divorce and remarriage, and (3) sexual lust against a woman. We will now consider each of these in order.

High Compliments

The Syro-Phoenician Woman (Matt. 15:28). This Gentile woman received one of the highest compliments known to have come from the lips of Jesus: "Oh woman, great is your faith," and it stands in stark contrast with the disciples' "little faith" only two chapters later (Matt. 17:20). The significant point in Matthew's account is that she was a Gentile, not that she was a woman, but it should not be lost that she addressed Jesus by a messianic title ("Son of David") and exhibited extraordinary humility toward him. Jesus rewarded her faith with healing.

The Poor Widow at the Temple (Mark 12:41-44=Luke 21:1-4). Both Mark and Luke's accounts come immediately after Jesus' stinging denunciation of the scribes for their open displays of self-importance, coupled with the charge that they "devour widows' houses." This indigent widow was so poor that she had nothing to devour, but that did not prevent her giving everything, "her entire living" (Mark 12:44). Jesus saw this as a teachable moment for his disciples, so he interpreted for them the significance of this woman's beautiful act. That he even noticed such an inconspicuous act in the midst of "large sums" (*polla*) being given by the wealthy speaks volumes about the way he looked compassionately on society's disenfranchised, in this case a destitute widow.

The Woman Who Anointed Jesus for His Burial (Matt. 26:6-13=Mark 14:3-9). Matthew (26:8) identifies those who were indignant at this woman's extravagant gift as "the disciples." Jesus' rebuke in her defense pointed out that she, not they, had her priorities straight. Little did they know that in two days his body would be laid in a tomb, and she was preparing it for that occurrence. It is at this point that Jesus pays her a compliment unparalleled in all the Gospels and one that transcends both space and time. "Wherever the gospel is preached in the whole world, what she has done will also be spoken in her memory" (Matt. 26:13=Mark 14:9).

Divorce and Remarriage

HERE THE DISCUSSION WILL BE LIMITED TO FOUR POINTS Jesus made that, because his position was counter-cultural, give us an indication of his uniquely sympathetic way of viewing women.

No Divorce from the Beginning (Matt. 19:8). The Pharisees who approached Jesus on the subject of divorce in Matthew 19 and Mark 10 believed that a man could divorce his wife, based on Deut. 24:1. The only point of dispute among them was what reasons could legitimize a divorce. One of Jesus' points in response to their question was that Gen. 1:27 and 2:24 trump Deut. 24:1. The latter was a concession by God due to the hardness of their hearts, but God's will since the beginning has been to oppose divorce.

The Current Practice of Multiple Reasons for Divorce Is Wrong (Matt. 5:32, 19:3, 6; Mark 10:9). Presumably since Deut. 24:1 permitted divorce, the Pharisees' question to Jesus in Matthew's account revolved around the possible justifications for a man to divorce his wife. "Is it lawful to divorce one's wife *for any cause*" (*kata pasan aitian*, 19:3)? The Pharisees disagreed among themselves as to whether the "cause" had a wide range of meanings or was limited to sexual impropriety. For Jesus, in the context of Deut. 24:1, the only acceptable cause for a man to divorce his wife was her unchastity (*porneia*, 19:9). It is clear from the Mishnah that the common practice in Palestine at the time was much more liberal than that, giving women very limited protections. The great Jewish rabbinics scholar C. G. Montefiore, in his commentary on Matthew (1970, p. 47), singles out Jesus' strict stance on divorce as one of the most notable areas where he believes Jesus stood out in his attitude toward women.

The Ability to Divorce One's Spouse Is Not Limited to Husbands (Mark 10:12). In his version of the dispute with the Pharisees over divorce, Mark records a subsequent exchange between Jesus and his disciples "in the house." Although in his statement to the Pharisees Jesus made it clear that he opposed all divorce, here in the house he taught his disciples that women and men were on an equal footing in dissolving a marriage relationship: ". . . and *if having divorced her husband* she marries another, she commits adultery." As we learned in chapter six, according to the Mishnah it was impossible for a woman to divorce her husband.

Adultery Can Be against the Wife, Not Just against the Husband. According to Jesus, the sanctity of the original marriage of a woman whose husband divorces her is so great that for him to marry a second woman is an act of adultery "against her" (*ep' autēn*) (Mark 10:11). This was unheard of among the rabbis, for whom adultery was seen as an offence to the married husband. How different was Jesus' view of marriage for both the man and the woman based on his dedication to God's will "from the beginning."

Sexual Lust against a Woman (Matt. 5:28)

WHEN JESUS SPOKE HERE OF A MAN COMMITTING ADUL-tery with a woman in his heart, this saying would have resonated well with the rabbis. To this point, Mary Evans (1983, p. 45) argues convincingly that while Jesus and the rabbis agreed that sexual lust was sin, they differed on whether it was inevitable. The rabbis avoided contact with women because of the ever-present problem of lust. Jesus did not tell his disciples not to look at women; he assumed they could control their lust and told them not to look at women lustfully.

It would be hard to overstate the significance of this point. The rabbis were so concerned about the dangers contact with women posed to their ability to avoid the sin of sexual lust that they erected barriers to cut down on that social interaction. According to Montefiore (p. 41), "to talk to a woman, to look at a woman, indeed to have anything to do with a woman, was regarded as dangerous and objection-able." Jesus rejected the idea that sexual lust was inevitable.

To him it was a choice. It has been suggested plausibly that Jesus' high standards about men controlling their lust and about divorce are what enabled him to associate freely with women and expect his disciples to intermingle the way they did without endangering their reputation.

Jesus' Association with Women

His Interactions with Them

IT IS NOTEWORTHY THAT THERE WAS NO DIFFERENCE between the way Jesus interacted with women than with men. Men and women were both treated as persons without gender becoming an issue. We see this in Jesus' healing ministry, in his sensitivity and compassion toward both, and in his willingness to discuss deep spiritual truths with both. He counted a number of women among his closest disciples. Because of women's low position, Jesus' treatment of them had the effect of greatly elevating their status. Here are some of the unique features of Jesus' association with women when viewed in the context of his day.

Jesus Interacted Freely with Women. Note some of these interactions in the Gospel of Luke. On one occasion Jesus joined the funeral procession of a widow's only son, raised him from the dead, and "gave him to his mother" (7:11-15). On another, at a meal in Simon the Pharisee's house, he allowed a woman of the city to touch him, forgave her sins and told her so, and then announced, "Your faith has saved you; go in peace" (7:36-50). On a preaching tour in Galilee, a group of women disciples traveled with him (8:2-3). He shared a meal with Martha and Mary in their home (10:38-40). On one Sabbath Jesus endured the rebuke of the ruler of a synagogue by touching a woman who had been ill for 18 years and healing her (13:10-17). Finally, in his most difficult hour as he was being led to the cross Jesus noticed a number of women weeping for him. He turned and spoke to them directly (23:27-31).

Jesus Had Physical Contact with Women, Touching Them and Allowing Them to Touch Him

Touching Women. The Gospels record at least three times that Jesus took a woman by the hand or laid his hands on her when he healed her. The first was when he healed Peter's mother-in-law from a fever (Matt. 8:15=Mark 1:31). Then he healed Jairus' twelve-year-old daughter (Matt. 9:25=Mark 5:41-42=Luke 8:54). Finally, on a Sabbath, Jesus healed a woman who had had a spirit of infirmity for 18 years (Luke 13:13).

Allowing Women to Touch Him. Of the four examples to be mentioned here, three were when Jesus' body was being anointed in a home. They are all indications of his remarkable comfort level with being touched by a woman in a totally asexual way. One was six days before his last Passover, presumably in the home of Martha, Mary and their brother Lazarus (John 12:1-3). Then just two days before that same Passover in the house of Simon the leper, an unidentified woman anointed Jesus' head with an expensive ointment (Matt. 26:6-13=Mark 14:3-9), with Jesus strong blessing.

The most remarkable anointing occurred earlier in his ministry. A sinner woman of the city interrupted a meal at the home of Simon the Pharisee. She knelt at Jesus' feet, and while she was sobbing washed his feet with her tears, dried them with her hair, and only then anointed them with ointment she had brought (Luke 7:36-38, 44-50). In what for any other rabbi would certainly have been an embarrassing and compromising situation, Jesus displayed no discomfort with her actions at all, calling particular attention to the intimacy of her physical contact with him (7:45). Finally, at the tomb the two Marys were greeted by Jesus, and "they coming up took hold of his feet and worshiped him" (Matt. 28:9).

There is also the matter of ceremonial uncleanliness brought on by physical contact. Jesus put ministering to people ahead of maintaining ceremonial cleanliness. The interaction with the woman with a flow of blood is a case in point (Matt. 9:20-22=Mark 5:25-34=Luke 8:43-48). According to Lev. 15:25-30, she was unclean, and contact with certain things she had touched could render him unclean for at least the rest of the day. However, instead of expressing concern that he had been violated by being rendered unclean by her touching him, he tenderly responded to her: "Daughter, your faith has rescued you. Go in peace, and be healed of your disease" (Mark 5:34).

Another example involves Jesus' interaction with the woman at the well (John 4). One passage in the Mishnah indicates that from birth a Samaritan woman was as unclean as a Jewish woman who was menstruating, meaning that she was always unclean. Touching a vessel that had been used by an unclean person also rendered one unclean, so Jesus was associating with a woman considered ritually unclean and was asking to use a vessel she had touched. These two examples show that Jesus did not allow the possibility of being rendered ritually unclean to prevent him from ministering freely to women.

Jesus Had a Committed Group of Female Disciples. Jesus had many (*pollai*) female disciples (Luke 8:3; Matt. 27:55=Mark 15:41). On one of his evangelistic tours through Galilee, the only disciples Luke mentions, other than the twelve, is a group of women in his entourage (8:2-3). The prominence of at least some of them is seen in the fact that they are mentioned by name. They were women of some means and so were able to provide support (*diakoneō*) for Jesus' traveling band. Later we find a large group of female Galilean disciples witnessing Jesus' crucifixion from a distance, and again their financial assistance to him is mentioned (Matt. 27:55-56=Mark 15:40-41). Note finally, how Mary Magdalene addressed Jesus at the tomb as "Rabboni" (John 20:16).

Jesus Taught Women. The Gospels make it clear that Jesus taught his female disciples just as he did his male followers. On one occasion, Mary, the sister of Martha and Lazarus, sat at the feet of Jesus while he was teaching (Luke 10:39), a rather unusual activity for a woman.

Two other passages, however, offer a better glimpse of the content of Jesus' teaching to some of his female disciples. The first involves Martha, Mary's sister (John 11:25-27). There are two parts to this encounter. Jesus first revealed to her a message found nowhere else in the Gospels. "I am the resurrection and the life. The one who believes in me, though he die, will live" (11:25). But this was not the first time he had taught her a profound truth, as is evidenced by her response to his question about whether she believed him. "Yes, Lord. I have come to believe that you are the Christ, the Son of God who is coming into the world" (11:27). Where but from Jesus would she have been taught this? Here she betrays a remarkable and accurate understanding of Jesus' true identity, which clearly indicates that she had been the recipient of some of Jesus' most intimate teaching.

The second instance occurred at the empty tomb, where at least three of Jesus' Galilean female disciples encountered two men (Luke 24:6-7). They reminded the women that back in Galilee Jesus had taught them that "The Son of man must be handed over into the hands of sinful men, and be crucified, and on the third day rise." This message was so private and sensitive that Jesus did not even consider his closest disciples ready for it until their retreat in the region of Caesarea Philippi (Matt. 16:21=Mark 8:31). Yet in time, Jesus taught the same message to some of his women disciples.

Perhaps the most remarkable example of Jesus teaching a woman was his encounter with the Samaritan woman at the well (John 4). Jesus shared with her at least four spiritual truths found here either for the first time on record or the only time in the Bible. The first dealt with living or running water (4:10, 13-14). The second concerned the spiritual character of God: "God is spirit," a revelation not found explicitly stated elsewhere in the Bible (4:24). Closely associated with this is the third—the spiritual nature of true worship: "the true worshippers will worship the Father in spirit and truth. . . . Those who worship Him must worship in spirit and truth" (4:23-24). Only here in the Gospels did Jesus disclose this to anyone, and remarkably it is to a woman and an outsider. Finally, here for the first time in the Gospels Jesus revealed to this woman that he was the Messiah (4:25-26). From these few examples we learn that Jesus was not inhibited by custom when it came to teaching women.

Jesus Defended Women. The Gospels record a few instances where Jesus came to the defense of women against hostile men. The greatest hostility came when a group of scribes and Pharisees at the Temple brought forward an adulteress and defiantly asked Jesus to pass judgment on whether she should be stoned or not (John 8:2-11). Rather than arguing the interpretation of Lev. 20:10 and Deut. 22:22-24 with them or asking them to produce her adulterous partner whom the Law said should also be executed, he skillfully confronted them with their own sinfulness. To the woman he offered no condemnation but rather a plea to reform her life. In another case, where Jesus healed a woman who had been chronically ill for 18 years, his response to the ruler of the synagogue concerned his hypocrisy in not recognizing the worth of a daughter of Abraham (Luke 13:10-17).

Three other examples involve women who anointed Jesus in different homes. First, at a meal at Simon the Pharisee's house, Jesus strongly defended the actions of a woman of the city who was a sinner (Luke 7:36-50). In his answer to Simon's judgmental thoughts, Jesus highlighted three ways the woman showed him greater respect and hospitality than he had. Jesus then capped his praise for her with the comment, "I tell you, her many sins are forgiven because she loved much. But the one who is forgiven little, loves little" (7:47). The second occurrence involved anointing Jesus' feet by his friend, Mary, and Jesus' rebuke of Judas for his criticism of her (John 12:1-8). Then, only a few days later in the home of Simon the leper, an unnamed woman incurred the criticism of the disciples for anointing Jesus' head with expensive ointment (Matt. 26:6-13=Mark 14:3-9). Jesus' response to this criticism forever memorialized her selfless act: "wherever this gospel is preached in the whole world, what she has done will also be spoken of in her memory."

Their Interactions with Him

WE NOW TURN TO THE INTERACTIONS BETWEEN JESUS and women from their point of view. We have already seen that he had a committed group of "many" female disciples in Galilee who chose to travel with and support him in his evangelistic work (Luke 8:1-3). Martha and Mary were Judean disciples who invited Jesus into the intimacy of their home on at least three occasions (Luke 10: 38; John 11:1ff., 12:1-3). Even more telling are the actions of a loyal group of women we encounter at the cross and the tomb.

Anyone who has read the Passion Narratives carefully has probably been struck by the fear, doubt, and downright cowardice of the male disciples, especially the twelve, during this time. The Gospels place only one male disciple anywhere near the cross (John 19:26-27), but many (*pollai*) of Jesus' female disciples from Galilee were there watching from a distance (Matt. 27:55-56=Mark 15:40-41=Luke 23:49). In addition, four women, including Jesus' mother, stood by the cross to the very end (John 19:25-30). The story of the women at the cross and at the tomb, then, deserves a closer look.

The Women at the Cross. Pilate's wife interceded on Jesus' behalf (Matt. 27:19), while her husband took the coward's way out (Matt. 27:24; John 18:38b, 19:12-16). On the way to the cross Jesus had a remarkable interaction with women in the crowd who were "lamenting and weeping for him" (Luke 23:27). Here, in his darkest hour, he turned and acknowledged this act of compassion and spoke to them (23:28-31). While Jesus was still alive, four women stood "by the cross" close enough to converse with him (John 19:25-27). In fact, a number of Jesus' female disciples who had followed him to Jerusalem from Galilee observed both what happened at the cross and some of them at least where his body was laid (Matt. 27:55-56=Mark 15:40-41=Luke 23:49, 55). Coupling this with the fact that a few women were the first to visit Jesus' tomb on resurrection Sunday, it appears that women were the last at the cross and the first at the empty tomb.

The Women at the Tomb. The Gospels are uniform in recording that certain women were the first and only people at the tomb at the beginning of resurrection morn. The central figure was Mary Magdalene. The testimony of the Gospel of John to her participation in the events of that day tells a remarkable story. She was the first at the tomb (20:1), the first to proclaim the empty tomb (20:2), the first to see and converse with the resurrected Jesus (20:14-17), and the first to bear witness to the resurrected Jesus (20:18), having been commissioned by Jesus himself to deliver the news to the disciples (20:17). Thus Jesus entrusted the announcement of what would become the most fundamental tenet of the Christian faith—Jesus has been raised from the dead—to a woman.

Conclusions

WHAT ARE WE TO MAKE OF ALL THIS? THERE IS LITTLE TO distinguish Jesus' references to women and activities of their lives in his teachings from the teachings of the Palestinian rabbis in the Mishnah. However, in his teachings *about* women and his association *with* them and they with him, he broke the mold. It is not an exaggeration to say that here Jesus comes across as decidedly counter-cultural. In Mark, Jesus' observation about the sacrificial gift of the poor widow at the Temple follows immediately his denunciation of the scribes for devouring widows' houses. His stance on divorce and remarriage differs from that of the rabbis in the Mishnah on at least four counts, setting the stage for Paul's likewise strong stance against Christians initiating a divorce against their Christian spouses, attributing this teaching to Jesus himself (I Cor. 7:10-11). Finally, in his teaching on male sexual lust he differed sharply from the rabbis in his insistence that a man can control his lust. With this high standard in sexual matters and by his own example in dealing with women even in close relationships, Jesus made it possible to create a band of men and women disciples who could associate freely with one another without raising the suspicion of immorality. This paved the way for similar close relations between men and women in the church.

As for Jesus' interactions with women, he freely conversed with them both publicly and in private. He had close female friends and even accepted meal invitations from them in their homes. Many of his women disciples traveled with and supported him and the twelve as he toured Galilee preaching and evangelizing. He showed no revulsion or embarrassment when being lovingly touched by even a sinner woman. Nor did he express concern that he had been rendered unclean by a sick woman's touch. Unlike his rabbinic counterparts, he had a committed band of female disciples, and he shared with them certain of his most important teachings, some of them for the first or only time in the biblical record.

On more than one occasion Jesus defended a woman against hostile men, even his own disciples. Finally, he interacted and conversed with women on the way to the cross, while on the cross, and shortly after his resurrection. He could not have been more different from the scribes and Pharisees.

So what are we to make of these significant changes in the position of women that could affect the future church? First, they are in line with Jesus' general compassionate approach to other marginalized groups in his day. If, after his death, his disciples are to follow in the trajectory set by Jesus, the lives of many downtrodden or ostracized people, not just women, will change dramatically for the better. Secondly, there is no discernible difference in the way Jesus treated or regarded men or women. He called both male and female disciples and seems to have made no distinction in teaching them. The significance of this for the church is obvious. Jesus set the stage for this new view of women, and we see his vision carried out in the church in the first few decades after his departure. That story begins in the next chapter.

Discussion Questions

1. How significant do you think Jesus' teaching about men's sexual lust and his open association with women was for the spread of early Christianity?

2. What are some of Jesus' most important teachings that he shared with women, in some cases for the first or only time?

3. What contrasts do you see in the way the Gospels portray Jesus' female and male disciples during the events surrounding his death, burial, resurrection, and the days following?

4. As the early church was working out its stance toward its female disciples, what might they have found helpful in Jesus' example?

CHAPTER EIGHT

Galatians 3:28 and Ephesians 5:21-33

A ny serious consideration of Paul's contribution to the matter of women in the church, especially what they may or may not do in the assembly, must necessarily examine in depth the three Pauline passages where he treats women in the assembly: I Corinthians 11 and 14 and I Timothy 2. Unfortunately, that is where most studies on the topic begin and not a few of them end. However, there are other texts in his writings, as well as in Acts, that provide significant information to paint a fuller picture. This chapter will deal with two of them: Gal. 3:28 and Eph. 5:21-33.

Paul and Jesus

Paul was a serious student of Rabban Gamaliel I the Elder of Jerusalem (Acts 22:3), but on his conversion he transferred his allegiance to another rabbi—Jesus Christ. It makes sense, then, that his approach to matters relating to women would be more influenced by what he learned from and about Jesus than what he had earlier learned from Gamaliel, and the evidence bears that out.

Paul treats the matter of marriage and divorce among Christians much like Jesus' overall approach. In marriage, the husband and wife are on equal footing (I Cor. 7:2-5), and on the matter of Christians divorcing each other, they are simply not do to it, a directive that comes from the Lord (Jesus) himself (7:10-11).

It is in Paul's *relationship* with women, however, that we find the strongest echoes of Jesus' example. Paul had close female friends, and he interacted freely with them. He was quite inclusive of women as evangelistic co-workers whom he treated on a par with himself and any others (Rom. 16:3, 6, 12; Phil. 4:3). Not only was it expected that women be taught (I Cor. 14:31, 35; I Tim. 2:11, 5:4), they were also to be teachers (Tit. 2:3-5; cf. Acts 18:26). He paid high compliments to various women, including one who was his benefactor (Rom. 16:2), another who had risked her neck for him (16:4), and one who had shared prison with him (16:7). He referred to women in the warmest and most affectionate terms: "outstanding" (Rom. 16:7), "beloved" (6:12), and "my (surrogate) mother" (16:13). These sisters in Christ were integral to the spread of the Gospel and service to the church, just as the male disciples were. The path Paul laid out for the church in both his attitude and actions toward women looks remarkably similar to and just as counter-cultural as that of Jesus.

Galatians 3:28

There is neither Jew nor Greek; there is neither slave nor free; there is neither male and female, for you are all one in Christ Jesus.

FOR MANY, GAL. 3:28 IS THE SINGLE MOST IMPORTANT passage in the NT dealing with the position of women. To them it expresses Paul's social agenda to eliminate, or at the very least, minimize male-female distinctions in the church and home. Unfortunately, rather frequently it is used out of context to support meanings well beyond simply answering the questions, what does it say? and what did it mean (in context)?

Most interpreters agree that the verse has an explicit meaning that relates to the vertical relationship with Christ. In Galatians Paul is trying to counter Judaizing teachers who are attempting to force Jewish practices on new Gentile Christians as requirements of their new faith. Galatians 3 has an extended counter argument centered on Abraham. It culminates in 3:26 with the statement, "for you are all sons of God through faith in Christ Jesus." Rather than observance of the Jewish law as the vehicle to be in a relationship as a child of God, faith in Christ is the key. It is through baptism that this union with Christ has occurred and the result was clothing oneself with Christ (3:27) or, put another way, being one with/in Christ Jesus (3:28). Hence, the three pairs in the first part of 3:28 have to do with becoming one with Christ through faith and baptism.

Certainly Paul's explicit point is clear, but some have suggested that there is a secondary or implied social meaning as well. In fact, that secondary meaning is often treated as if it were the central Pauline teaching on women in the church and the family. In effect, these interpreters find more meaning in what Paul does not say (that is, what he is thought to have *implied*) than in what the text actually says. This is not to say that there are no social implications for these three groups related to their oneness with Christ. Paul specifies what they are elsewhere. We simply need to base our conclusions on those passages, not on what we subjectively find implicit in this verse. We now turn to one of those passages relating to men and women where Paul is explicit—Ephesians 5:21-33.

Ephesians 5:21-33

Literary, Social, and Biblical Contexts

THIS PASSAGE IS PART OF A LARGER ONE CONTINUING through 6:9. To understand it properly we need to set it in its literary, social, and biblical contexts.

Literary Context. Eph. 5:22-6:9 is a household code, a common literary type in Greco-Roman literature of the time. These codes cover the various relationships present in Roman households: husband-wife, father-children, and master-slave.

Social Context. While these three relationships are found in Roman homes, they go back ultimately to Aristotle in his *Politics*. Russ Dudrey's (1999, pp. 27-44) excellent treatment of these household relationships in the ancient Mediterranean world shows that according to Aristotle, *ruling* or *commanding* is what the man does, and the duty of the three subordinate roles (wives, children, slaves) is *obedience*. This was true in all the cultures with which the NT church interacted. Further, functionally throughout the culture women, children, and slaves were all treated as property of the father or husband. This family patriarch in the Roman world was known as *paterfamilias*.

Biblical Context. Ephesians has the most highly developed Ecclesiology (doctrine of the church) in the NT with Christology as it secondary theme. In the first three chapters, Paul argues that what Christ has done in bringing salvation to both Jews and Gentiles in one body was God's secret (*mysterion*) plan hidden from the ages. The recipients of the letter were members of the household of God (2:19), and chapters 4-6 tell them how to live as that household. The current passage,

5:22-6:9, instructs them on how to conduct themselves in their own households. When we compare this household code in Ephesians with similar ones in Colossians 3 and I Peter 2-3, the big difference is the eight verses Paul devotes to husbands in Ephesians 5, as opposed to one each in the other two. This is where Paul puts the emphasis, and this is where we should look to find his major point.

Exposition

Submit yourselves to one another out of reverence for Christ. (5:21)

Submit to One Another. Verse 21 serves as the heading for the household code that follows in 5:22-6:9. Although the matters of subordination to *authority* or *obedience* or *inferiority* may be present in some contexts where the verb "submit yourself" (*hupotassō*) is used in Paul, none of these is inherent in the verb itself. The household code in Eph. 5:21-6:9 has all of the six types of individuals submitting to one another (5:21); yet clearly children are not in a position of authority over their fathers (6:1), nor slaves over their masters (6:5). Further, there are no NT examples of *hupotassō* referring to one person subjecting another. Submission to another is voluntary, never forced. In this case, what wives, husbands, children, fathers, slaves, and masters are asked to do is an expression of what Paul means by "submit yourselves to one another out of reverence for Christ" (5:21).

As any of the three weaker parties in the household code would have read how they were to behave, they would have found nothing new. What was new, however, was the motivation. Just as the motivation for all the parties to submit to one another was "out of reverence for Christ" (5:21), so in each case some aspect of their relationship with Christ was the motivation for their specific behavior, and that was totally new. In the case of the stronger parties (husbands, fathers, and masters), both the behavior and motivation for it were new. Christ has changed everything.

> *Wives to your own husbands as to the Lord. For the husband is head of the wife as Christ is head of the church, being himself Savior of the body. But as the church submits itself to Christ, so the wives also to their husbands in everything. . . . And the wife that she should respect her husband. (5:22-24, 33b)*

Wives. Several points stand out as we look at what wives are asked to do and why. First, they are to submit themselves to their husbands, something that in any culture at the time was understood. Note, however, that this is a voluntary act on the wives' part, and nothing in either Paul's instructions to the wives or to the husbands gives the husband the right to demand or enforce his wife's submission. Second, the motivation for the wife's submitting herself to her husband introduces what is totally new—"as to the Lord" (verse 22). Third, the word "head" (*kephalē*) in 5:23 in the statement "the husband is head of the wife" refers to his function as leader, just as the word is used of Christ here (5:23) and in Eph. 1:22 and Col. 1:18, 2:10. Fourth, wives are not told to obey their husbands, as children are their parents (6:1) and slaves are their masters (6:5), but rather to submit themselves to them. Something entirely different than autocratic rule is going on in Paul's view of marriage here. Finally, the nature of the husband's headship that Paul develops beginning in verse 25 is already indicated by what Paul says about Christ's headship of the church in verse 23. Rather than emphasizing Christ's authority over the church, Paul characterizes Christ's headship as what he lovingly did for the church in becoming its Savior.

Husbands, love your wives as Christ also loved the church and gave himself up for her, that he might consecrate her by cleansing her in the washing of water by the word, that he might present the church to himself resplendent, not having spot or wrinkle or any of such things, but that she may be holy and unblemished. In this way husbands also ought to love their own wives as their own bodies. He who loves his own wife loves himself. For no one has ever hated his own body, but he nourishes and cherishes it, as Christ also does the church, because we are members of his body. . . . Let each one of you individually in this way love his own wife as himself. (5:25-30, 33a)

Husbands. So, Paul's revolutionary description of what the husband's headship looks like does not involve the exercise of his authority over his wife or treating her as a personal possession or regarding her as one to be ruled or commanded, as would be common in his culture. Paul says she is to be loved. And he is very explicit about what that means. It involves an entirely different kind of headship, one defined by Christ's love for his church. Further, he identifies the characteristics of Christ's love for the church that the husband is to emulate and turns them into what Christ expects of the husband in turn. Love for one's wife is to go as far as to give his life for her (5:25), to be as intense as for his own body or self (5:28, 33), and to be serving ("nourish and cherish," 5:29)—all based on the way Christ expressed his love for the church. This is the way a Christian husband lives out the words, "Submit yourselves to one another out of reverence for Christ" (5:21).

Galatians 3:28 and Ephesians 5:21-33 Taken Together

WHEN WE CONSIDER GAL. 3:28 AND EPH. 5:21-33 together, we find that the latter passage helps correct a common misuse of the former. That misuse is a questionable application (answering the question, what *does* it mean?) of the verse that Paul himself does not make. Some interpreters see the verse as signaling a reversal of a consequence of Adam and Eve's sin, effectively wiping out a "hierarchical" relationship between husbands and wives.

This does not mean that Paul does not have something liberating to say about the relationship of married Christians. This is where Eph. 5:21-33 comes in. It, not Gal. 3:28, is where Paul develops the effect of the gospel on gender relations within marriage. Rather than negating the so-called hierarchical relationship between Christian husbands and wives, he shows how Christ's sacrifice has totally redirected the relationship. Wives are still to submit themselves to their husbands (5:22-24, 33b), but Jesus is now brought into the picture as the reason. Paul goes even farther with Christian husbands by mandating a love that transcends mere feeling into action that is based on the model of Christ's sacrificial giving for his beloved bride.

What Paul does here, rather than applying the gospel to wipe out any hierarchical relationship that may be a remnant of the creation story, is to so elevate the status of the wife in a Christian marriage as effectively to nullify any advantage or imbalance in the relationship held by the husband. In this passage there is no trace of ruling or any other form of domination by the husband. In its place is serving ones wife in unprecedented ways based on an unprecedented foundation—Christ's love for his bride as demonstrated by what he has *done* for her. This is far more powerful than the supposed removal of hierarchy by a questionable interpretation of Gal. 3:28. It puts the responsibility for the relationship on both parties and provides the motivation to make it work.

But in going back to Gal. 3:28, what about the third question (what *does* it mean?) for those of us who live after the NT? Some have suggested that the situation with males and females in marriage in the NT world is similar to that with slavery. Their point is that with slavery, the later church has been able to apply the gospel in ways that were not possible in the first century.

Few Christians today would argue that it is acceptable to take away other people's freedom by personally owning them. Yet the NT does not condemn this practice; rather it "baptized" it into Christ. Slave owners and slaves alike had new responsibilities imposed on them by what Christ had done for them. Many have suggested plausibly that the reason Paul and others in the NT did not oppose slavery directly is that it was just too much a part of the social fabric. Christians were a fragile, infant movement that had to pick its battles carefully. The survival of the movement was at stake. Also, their ability to reach an already suspicious populous with the gospel message was a major concern. Hints of the final destination were already there in NT passages that changed the way Christians were to act toward their slaves and in Philemon, where Paul went about as far as he could without insisting that Philemon free Onesimus. But it was left to Christians in more stable and favorable times to take on this battle.

Is it possible that for the relationship between Christian husbands and wives the last chapter had not been written in Paul's day for similar reasons than were true of slavery? Are there hints in the NT that point to a more egalitarian relationship in marriage, to use a modern term? Gal. 3:28 and I Cor. 11:11-12 are certainly possible candidates, as is the lack of any clear reference in Paul to Gen. 3:16 as the source of his teaching on wives' subordination to their husbands.

The most that can be said here is that although the answer must begin by being faithful to the findings from the first two questions, it is really a matter of addressing the third. Certainly, just as it was in the case of slavery, for many it may be worth their effort to pursue the question of what *does* it mean in our modern world. My two caveats are these. First, this present book is concerned primarily with what the biblical text says and meant in Paul's day. For Paul, the author of Gal. 3:28, for whatever his reasons, wives were still to be submissive to their husbands (Eph. 5:22-24). Secondly, for me the above analysis of Paul's teaching about husbands' responsibilities to their wives renders the effort to mitigate the effect of wives' submission to their husbands unnecessary, even counterproductive for wives. Speaking as a Christian husband, when I read Ephesians 5 and ask the third question—what *does* it mean for me and my behavior toward my wife?—, it elevates her needs and wellbeing above my own. From my perspective, that is a different kind of hierarchy, but one that is much weightier on me than on her.

Discussion Questions

1. What is Paul's point in Gal. 3:28?

2. Where does Paul put the emphasis in his treatment of the household code in Eph. 5:22-6:9?

3. What, if anything, can we learn from the NT treatment of slavery and its modern application that can help us apply NT teaching to women in the church today?

4. What are the dangers of treating biblical passages in "proof text" fashion?

CHAPTER NINE

I Corinthians 11:2-16

We are now ready to examine the first of the three NT passages that have had the most influence on the role of women in the church down to our day. All three are in Paul (I Cor. 11:2-16, 14:34-35, and I Tim. 2:8-15). It is no exaggeration to say that were it not for these three passages the history of women in the church would have been written very differently. If you remove these passages from the mix, there is nothing in the NT that would cause one to suspect there are any restrictions on what women may do in Christian assemblies. In fact, these three passages, especially the latter two, move against the flow of NT teaching about the status and role of women in congregational life. Further, when we consider Jesus' example and teachings discussed in chapter seven of this book, we are again struck by how foreign these three Pauline texts sound. Nevertheless, these passages are difficult and filled with many ambiguities caused by our ignorance of elements of the setting against which they were written. Good, well-trained, dedicated and sincere Christians can be found on all sides of the issue. It is not helpful to question the motives of those with whom we disagree, because the complexity of these passages is such that it is possible to hold the Bible in high regard as our final authority and disagree on particulars in them.

Introduction

I Cor. 11:2-16 presents the modern reader with almost insurmountable interpretive difficulties. Not only are we in the dark at every turn on statements that are inexplicable without the aid of knowledge of the historical, linguist and cultural background, but the matters discussed find parallels in almost no other Pauline, not to mention biblical, passages. So as not to get bogged down in issues that are peripheral to our focus on women in the church, the discussion here will be limited to answering five questions: (1) what is the setting being addressed, (2) who are the man and woman in 11:3b, (3) what is their relationship, (4) what activities in that setting are being addressed and what restrictions are placed on them, and (5) how wide-spread was the application of those restrictions among sister congregations.

The Key Questions

The Setting

11:2 begins a long, multi-chapter section that deals with the regular Corinthian assemblies. The overall section concerns three problem areas in the assembly: (1) head coverings while engaging in praying and prophesying (11:2-16), (2) abuses of fellow Christians in the observance of the Lord's Supper (11:17-34), and (3) disorderly conduct in the exercise of spiritual gifts in the assembly (chapter 14). Even the discussion of spiritual gifts addressed in chapters 12 and 13 prepares the reader for Paul's treatment of how they are to be exercised when the church comes together for worship (chapter 14). Seven times in this four-chapter section

Paul refers to the church coming together (*sunerchomai*) (11:17, 18, 20, 33, 34, 14:23, 26), in two of which (11:18 and 14:23) he specifically mentions the assembly (*ekklēsia*). The specific connection of the discussion of head covering in 11:2-16 and the Lord's Supper in 11:17-34 is evident from the introductory words of each section ("I commend," 11:2 and "I do not commend," 11:17). All of this strongly suggests that what Paul is dealing with in 11:2-16 is the regular Corinthian assembly.

The Man and Woman in 11:3b

. . . and the head of a woman/wife is the man/husband (11:3b)

PAUL BEGINS THIS SECTION ON HEAD COVERINGS IN THE assembly with a statement unlike any other in the Bible. "Now I want you to know that. . . the head of a woman/ wife is the man/husband" (11:3). Here we encounter one of the major interpretive difficulties of this passage in that the words for "woman" (*gunē*) and "man" (*anēr*) may mean either "woman" or "wife" and "man" or "husband." Translators are divided on how to render these words in this verse. However, the question is larger than simply Paul's meaning in 11:3, because *gunē* occurs 15 additional times in 11:2-16, more than in any other passage of comparable length in Paul. Thus, the issue is whether the passage as a whole, beginning with 11:3, is best seen as referring to married women or women in general. There are at least six reasons to conclude that Paul has husbands and wives in mind.

First, although the exact custom in Paul's Corinth is unknown, in general the wearing of a head covering in the Mediterranean world was associated with *married* women.

Second, up to this point in I Corinthians, *anēr* had always meant husband (16 times); *gunē* had meant wife (21 times) in all but two of its occurrences (7:1, 34). Thus, the natural way for Paul's readers to have interpreted these words in 11:3-15 is as referring to husbands and wives.

Third, the only other passage in Paul where *anēr* is said to be head (*kephalē*) of *gunē* is Eph. 5:23, which is specifically discussing husbands and wives.

Fourth, Paul describes the three relationships in 11:3 in individual, rather than group terms. Note how Christ is not the head of men in general, but *of every man*. The same is true of the man and woman. Paul refers to *gunē* and *anēr* in the singular, not in the plural as men and women. Thus, just as with the other two relationships in 11:3, Paul envisions the relationship between the man and the woman as individual and person to person. This is reinforced in 11:4-5, where the conduct of *every* man and *every* woman (not *men* and *women*) might dishonor their head. Even the reference to "head" (*kephalē*) is not collective but individual (*his* head and *her* head).

Fifth, 11:8-9 draws on the creation narrative and refers to a married couple, the first one, and their specific relationship with each other. Nothing in these two verses could refer to a generic relationship between men and women.

Finally, to the extent that 11:3 affirms a hierarchal relationship between the three pairs, this would point decisively toward husband and wife, not man and woman generically. Nothing in Paul or in any of the rest of the Bible puts men in general in a hierarchal relationship with women in general. Where there is a hierarchy, it is only in the family (husband-wife, father-daughter). If 11:3b were referring to men and women in general, rather than to a husband and his wife, it would run counter to the rest of the Bible, including the creation account. Therefore, the overwhelming probability is that Paul has husbands and wives in view in 11:3 and the passage overall. Consequently, this passage is misused when it is taken to refer to men and women generically in the church.

The Relationship between the Man and the Woman

Every wife praying or prophesying with her head uncovered dishonors her head . . . . The wife is the glory of the husband. . . . Neither is the wife without the husband, nor the husband without the wife in the Lord. (11:5a, 7c, 11)

FROM THE WIFE'S SIDE OF THE EQUATION, WHETHER OR not she covered her head while praying or prophesying in the assembly directly affected her husband, "her head" (11:5). She dishonored him if she did not cover her head. Though many interpreters read subordination into the passage, that is not Paul's point at all. The reason for her to cover her head is not that she should submit herself to him (*hupotassō*, "to submit," appears nowhere in the passage), but rather the positive thought that she is his glory (11:7c). Then in 11:11 Paul says that nevertheless "in the Lord" there is a beautiful mutuality in their relationship. "Neither is the wife without the husband, nor the husband without the wife."

Activities and Restrictions on Them

Every husband praying or prophesying having his head covered dishonors his head. But every wife praying or prophesying with her head uncovered dishonors her head. . . . For a husband ought not to cover his

head, since he is the image and glory of God. . . . Is it
fitting for a wife to pray to God uncovered?
(11:4-5a, 7a-b, 13)

IN THESE VERSES ONLY TWO ACTIVITIES FOR BOTH MEN
and women are under consideration (praying and prophesying, 11:4-5, 13) and only one restriction (that on head covering or lack of it for both women and men, 11:4-7, 13). Let's
look at these two activities and one restriction a little closer.

Activities. We should not allow the massive amount of smoke
that has been generated around these verses obscure the one
simple teaching here. Both men and women prayed and
prophesied in Christian meetings in Corinth, and the only distinction between the two was their head covering. Yet, many
interpreters interject elements that go well beyond what Paul
wrote in the text. For example, some suggest that the women's
prayer was silent, with others leading. Other than the fact that
the passage says no such thing, why do these interpreters not
make the same claim about the men's prayers? Further, women
not only prayed, but they prophesied. Prophecy, by its very
nature is spoken out loud to others. If women did that in the
assemblies, why should they be forbidden to pray out loud?
In short, Paul makes no distinction between what women
and men did (*what* they did, *how* they did it, *where* they did
it, etc.) other than the matter of head covering.

Restrictions on Them. Although a few modern students
of this passage see the head covering in 11:4-7, 13 to be the
man or woman's hair, by far the majority of interpreters, for
good reason, believe that Paul has in mind a covering over
the hair or head. Richard Oster's groundbreaking article
on this passage (1988, pp. 481-505) describes this. First, he
notes that Paul is concerned with the head covering or lack

of it for *both* men and women. He explains that at the time Paul wrote I Corinthians Corinth was a Roman colony and in certain respects was more Roman than Greek. One of these was in worship settings, where Romans covered their heads during such acts as prayer, sacrifice, and prophecy. According to Oster, the gesture of covering the head during a worship activity "consisted of pulling part of one's garment or toga over the back of the head and then forward until it approached or covered the ears" (p. 496). Paul's wording in 11:4, literally "having on the head" (*kata kephalēs echōn*), matches that gesture perfectly.

For this reason the wife ought to have authority on her head, because of the angels. (11:10)

THE FINAL MATTER RELATING TO A POTENTIAL RESTRIC-tion on women in the assembly arises in 11:10, where Paul writes, ". . . the wife ought to have authority on her head, because of the angels." This verse has baffled readers for centuries, especially the reference to angels, but for our purpose here it is not the angels, but the word, "authority" (*exousia*), that requires our attention. So what does Paul mean when he uses the word "authority" in this context?

Does *exousia* mean authority that a woman has or, as many assert, the authority of another that she is under? An examination of Paul's 26 uses of *exousia* provides strong evidence for the former, namely, the authority a woman has. Paul uses the word 14 times of those who are in positions of authority, clearly not relevant to his use here in 11:10. All of the other 11 occurrences, excluding the one here in 11:10, have to do with one's right or authority over something or to do something. Thus, if Paul is here using the word as he does in every other similar case, the authority resting on a woman's head is her authority or right to do something.

How, then, does this fit the context in 11:2-16? Here is one suggestion. While in that cultural setting, unlike our own, it could be shameful (*aischron*) for a wife to speak in a religious assembly (14:35), her right to do so in the form of praying or prophesying was signified by what was on her head (11:10). She did not have the right to be disruptive to the assembly (14:34-35), just as was the case with tongue speakers (14:27-28) and prophets (14:29-33), but her head covering gave her the right to pray and prophesy. In the final analysis, according to Paul in 11:2-16 the only restriction on a wife in the assembly was that she cover her head when she prayed and prophesied.

How Widespread the Restrictions Were Applied

We do not have such a custom, nor do the churches of God. (11:16)

THE USE OF *TOIAUTĒ* ("SUCH") IN THIS STATEMENT, RATHER than the Greek words for "other" or "different," suggests that the practice he is urging on the Corinthians (men with no head covering and women with head covering) is one that fits their particular cultural setting, rather than conforming to the practice in other churches. He is stating that the Corinthian practice was neither his own nor that of "the churches of God," i.e., the general practice elsewhere.

Many English versions mistranslate *toiautē* as "other," presumably because the translators find it difficult to believe that Paul would issue such a disclaimer when he has expended so much effort urging such particular directions on head coverings. However, this approach disregards the first question (what does it say?) and moves directly to the second (what did it mean?), leading to a complete misreading of what Paul actually wrote. There is, however, a way to take seriously what Paul *says* in this context. A reasonable explanation is that he wanted the Corinthians' practice to be sensitive to their cultural setting. If you want to be contentious (*philoneikos*) about it (11:16), you don't have to do it the way he was proposing. If, however, you are to be imitators of him as he was of Christ (11:1), you would forgo your freedom to do as you please. Paul's own practice relative to eating food sacrificed to idols and other matters was to forgo his freedom so as not to give offense to others and to bring the many to salvation (10:32-33; cf. 9:1-6, 12). It is at this point in the letter that he writes, "Become imitators of me just as I am also of Christ" (11:1).

This overall interpretation of 11:16 is further supported by two additional considerations. First, most interpreters today believe that Paul was not laying down a rule about head covering for every congregation for all time. It was a convention that made sense in the unique cultural setting in Roman Corinth. Thus, few interpreters today would use Paul's reference to "the churches of God" (11:16) to support the adoption of what the Corinthians were being asked to do about head covering as universally applicable today.

Secondly, Corinth is the only place we encounter instructions about head coverings in the assembly. In fact, there is evidence for a different practice in Ephesus. Everett Ferguson (2014, p. 242), in his excellent article on women's head-coverings in antiquity, observes that "the instructions about hairstyles in 1 Tim. 2:9 and 1 Pet. 3:3 imply women's heads were uncovered." If Ferguson is right, as seems reasonable, then Paul could hardly have meant in I Cor. 11:16 that his instructions about head covering for women in that passage reflect the uniform practice of "the churches of God."

Conclusions

IN SPITE OF THE LARGE NUMBER OF ELEMENTS OF THIS passage that present the modern reader with such difficulties, a few points come through rather clearly.

First, Paul's key concern is to convince the Corinthian men to keep their heads uncovered when they prayed or prophesied in the assembly and the women to cover theirs when they prayed or prophesied in the same setting. The reason was so as not to be so out of step with local custom that they would dishonor Christ or their husbands respectively.

Second, the context within the letter supports the conclusion that the activities described took place in the regular Corinthian assemblies. There is no basis in the text for assuming that Paul viewed men as performing these acts in one type of Christian meeting and the women in another. Nor is there any indication that men and women were not in the meetings together.

Third, in 11:3 and in the passage as a whole, Paul primarily has husbands and wives in mind, not men and women generically. Nothing, either in this passage, in Paul generally, or anywhere else in the Bible supports the view that God has placed men in general over women in general in any setting.

Fourth, the way Paul describes covering the head when he is talking about the man suggests that the covering he has in mind for both men and women is the toga pulled up over the head.

Fifth, what men and women were permitted to do in the assembly was exactly the same. They both prayed and prophesied out loud in these Christian meetings. The only difference was in their head covering or lack of it.

Sixth, it would seem that Paul's instructions for head covering for men and women reflected the unique cultural situation in Roman Corinth at the time. They were not the universal practice of the churches with which Paul was acquainted, nor were they intended to be the universal practice for every congregation for all time.

Discussion Questions

1. How does doing a concordance study help us determine the meaning of a word like "authority" in I Cor. 11:10?

2. Can you think of an example in the Bible where men in general, because they are men, are placed in a hierarchal position over women, because they are women?

3. What evidence is there in the text that Paul did not intend his instructions for head covering of men and women to be applied to all other churches?

4. If women prayed and prophesied out loud in the Corinthian assemblies (11:5), what is the justification for forbidding women to pray out loud in our assemblies today?

CHAPTER TEN

I Corinthians 14:34-35

We now turn to the short passage that contains the most widely used proof text in support of traditional limitations on what women may do in the assembly. Differences of opinion on these two verses are enormous. What follows is an examination of the key features of the passage that relate to the question of what women may or may not do in the Christian assembly.

The Text

THE PASSAGE CONTAINS TWO TEXTUAL VARIANTS THAT require consideration here, the most significant of which is the placement of 14:34-35 in chapter 14 itself. The other is the punctuation of 14:33.

Placement of 14:34-35

A FEW INTERPRETERS QUESTION THE PAULINE AUTHORSHIP of these two verses based on the fact that, although none of the manuscript tradition leaves them out entirely, a small number of Western manuscripts put 14:34-35 after 14:40. However, given the extremely weak manuscript evidence for placing these two verses after 14:40, taking the next step by denying their Pauline authorship is quite a stretch.

These interpreters also argue that the two verses do not

fit well in the context and intrude on the flow of Paul's argument. Certainly, if the reader focuses on tongue speaking and prophesying as Paul's primary interest in this chapter, then the two verses might seem out of place with no easy explanation for them. However, when one recognizes that *edification* and *order* during the assembly were Paul's concern and tongue speaking and prophesying were his cases in point, then the placement of these two verses where the vast majority of the manuscript evidence puts them makes perfect sense. Thus, in view of the weight of the manuscript evidence and compatibility with the context, these two verses should be regarded both as correctly placed at 14:34-35 and genuinely Pauline.

Punctuation of 14:33

SINCE ANCIENT GREEK MANUSCRIPTS OF THE NT DO NOT contain punctuation, translators do not always agree on when one thought ends and another begins. I Cor. 14:33 is one of those passages. Does "as in all the churches of the saints" go with what precedes or what follows? English translations are fairly evenly divided, so factors within the biblical text itself must be considered to make an informed judgment.

Goes with What Follows. 14:36, immediately after the women's section, reads, "Or did the word of God go out from you, or did it reach you only"? Some see this reference to "*you only*" as set in opposition to "*all* the churches" in 14:33b. This would mean that 14:33b and 14:36 would frame 14:34-35, making it a self-contained unit. On the other hand, there is good reason instead to take 14:36 with the next verse, where the reference to "prophet" and "spiritually gifted" points back to all of chapter 14, and "a command of the Lord" may be a critique of the presumptiveness expressed in 14:36.

Goes with What Precedes. There are at least three good reasons to take 14:33b as completing the thought in 14:33a. First, the earliest known evidence supports the conclusion that 14:33b does not go with what follows. The fourth century Sinaiticus manuscript has a break between 14:33 and 14:34, not between 14:33a and 14:33b. Further, the Western manuscripts and versions that place the women's section after 14:40 (see discussion above) do not include "as in all the churches of the saints." Finally, Chrysostom's (ca. 347-407) *Homily 36 on First Corinthians* disconnects 14:33b from the woman' passage. Second, if 14:33b ("as in all the *churches* of the saints") and 14:34a ("let the women be silent in the *churches*") made up the same sentence, an awkward, though not impossible, redundancy would be created with the repetition of the word "churches" (*ekklēsia*). Third, in all three of the other places in I Corinthians where Paul makes a similar statement (4:17, 7:17, and 11:16), the words conclude the previous thought rather than begin the following one. Thus, it seems more likely that 14:33b should not be taken as a part of the woman's passage in 14:34-35, though certainty is impossible. However, it makes no difference to the question of its applicability to the matter of women in the church. Paul's teaching here would apply anywhere else the conditions that prevailed in Corinth at that time also existed.

Exposition

Let the women/wives be silent in the assemblies/ churches (14:34a)

OTHER THAN GAL. 3:28, NO PASSAGE RELATING TO WOMEN in the church has been detached from its context and treated as a proof text more frequently than this statement: "let the

women be silent in the churches." Let's begin by looking
at the context, which is the need for order in the assembly
(14:27, 31, 40) or, expressed another way, the lack of disorder
(14:33a). The same corrective for disorder created by some of
the tongue speakers and prophets—silence (*sigao*)—is prescribed for certain women who were interrupting the flow of
the assembly with their persistent questions when they had a
better alternative for getting them answered. In context, the
silence required of these tongue speakers and prophets pertains to the point of order under consideration. Who would
argue that they were also forbidden to speak in other respects
in the assembly simply because of this requirement for silence?
Why should it have been any different for these women?

Paul leaves no doubt that the offenders were certain married women. That the women (wives) who have "their own
husbands" in 14:35 are the same as the women who are to
be silent 14:34 could not be clearer. Note the unmistakable
grammatical connection. "Let the women/wives (*gunē*) be
silent in the assemblies/churches, for it is not permitted for
them (*autais*) to speak, but let *them* submit themselves, just as
the law says. But if *they* want to learn something, let *them* ask
their own husbands at home, for it is shameful for a woman/
wife to speak in the assembly." Thus, there is no justification
for reading "women" (*gunē*) in 14:34 or "woman" (*gunē*) in
14:35 generically as women, rather than as wives.

It is unclear why Paul singled out these wives for the
same restriction he put on tongue speakers and prophets,
but there are at least two possible explanations. First, they
were the only ones disrupting the order in the assembly
in this way. Had anyone else, even some of the men, been
guilty of what they were doing, Paul would have included
them, because his overriding concerns in this chapter
were *edification* and *order* in the assembly. It just happens

that these wives were the only ones who needed to be corrected for this particular conduct. Second, these wives had an advantage over other women. They had Christian husbands who were capable of answering questions about what went on in the assembly on a given day. In the case of these particular women, the solution was simple—ask your husbands at home rather than disrupting the assembly. This was a simple solution to a simple problem involving only a specific group of women.

For it is not permitted for them to speak, but let them submit themselves, just as the law also says (14:34b)

Speaking. We now turn from these wives being silent in the assembly, like the tongue speakers and prophets, to their speaking. Paul uses the common Greek word for speaking, *laleō*, twice in these two verses. The key point in understanding his use of this infinitive here is its tense. An infinitive in the present tense, the one Paul uses here, refers to the action as occurring repeatedly. Thus, Paul is not talking about these wives speaking up or asking their questions every once in a while. This was something they were repeatedly doing, and herein lay at least a part of the problem. In the context of order in the assembly (14:27, 31, 33, 40) such recurrent questioning of the speakers would have been disruptive to that order, so Paul asks that they stop doing it. To generalize this prohibition to all speaking in the assembly does not take adequate account of either the context or the force of this present infinitive for "speak."

Submitting Themselves. Here Paul employs the verb, *hupotassō* , "submit," of these women. In chapter eight of this book in the section "**Submit to One Another**," the following two points were made about how Paul uses this word.

First, although the matters of subordination to *authority* or *obedience* or *inferiority* may be present in some contexts where Paul uses the verb, none of these is inherent in the verb itself. For example, subordination to authority can hardly be involved in I Cor. 16:16, where Paul directs the Corinthians to submit to several people in the congregation, none of whom is indicated as having any kind of authority. Second, there are no NT examples of *hupotassō* referring to one person subjecting another. Submission is voluntary. It comes from within the person submitting, rather than being forced on him/her by another.

To whom these wives are to submit is, unfortunately, not stated. It could be to their husbands, the leaders of the congregation, other members of the congregation, the need of the congregation for order (see 14:27, 31, 33, 40), or something or someone else. The most that can be said here is that Paul is asking these wives to submit themselves to another/others by modifying their behavior in the assembly.

The Law (*ho nomos*). Paul's justification for asking these wives to submit themselves is "just as the law also says." Many have noted that nothing in "the law," assuming that "the law" refers to something in the OT, fits Paul's specific point here, and he does not provide any further information to help the modern reader determine the meaning. While it would be helpful to know exactly what Paul meant, unfortunately, we are too far removed from the world of Paul and the Corinthians to arrive at an understanding with any level of certainty. Therefore, it is better simply to say that in Paul's mind something in "the law," whatever he means by that, supported his instructions for these wives.

But if there is something they want to learn, let them ask their own husbands at home (14:35a)

THESE FEW WORDS OFFER THE KEY TO UNDERSTANDING what in these wives' behavior Paul wanted to stop when he silenced them. He is fairly clear about what he wanted to cease. These wives were repeatedly asking questions in the assembly that they could get answered elsewhere more appropriately without damaging order in the assembly. If they had a husband present who could teach them what they wanted to learn, they should wait until they get home to get their questions answered.

For it is shameful for a woman/wife to speak in an
assembly/church (14:35b)

PAUL OFFERS TWO REASONS IN SUPPORT OF HIS SILENCING OF these wives: the law, as it relates to their submitting themselves (14:34), and custom (*aischron*, "shameful," 14:35). Here we are concerned with the latter. The repeated speaking of these wives (present infinitive of *laleō*, "to speak") in that setting was regarded as shameful (*aischron*). As is widely recognized in both the literature and lexical tools, this adjective carries the nuance of culture-related shame. It represents the conduct of wives in public presumably when their husbands were present. In this sense, then, it is not unlike the cultural shame of having their heads shaved or shorn (*aischron*, "shameful") or failing to wear their head covering when they prayed or prophesied (*kataischunō*, "dishonor") that we encountered in 11:5-6. Thus, this second of Paul's reasons for silencing these wives has no bearing on cultural settings, like our own, where such a practice is not shameful.

I Corinthians 11:5 and 14:34

BEFORE SUMMARIZING THE CONCLUSIONS REACHED IN THIS chapter on I Cor. 14:34-35, one final matter needs attention. Almost everyone who writes on both I Cor. 11:2-16 and 14:34-35 calls attention to a supposed conflict between 11:5 and 14:34. The issue has to do with the apparent approval of women speaking in the assembly by praying and prophesying in 11:5 and disapproval of speaking in the assembly in 14:34.

Since 11:5 demonstrates that women did speak out loud (praying and prophesying) in the Corinthian assemblies, the key to solving this proposed conundrum may lie in what Paul means by "speak" in 14:34. Many interpreters take "it is not permitted for them to speak" as absolute, meaning that Paul is forbidding any kind of speaking in the assembly. Additionally, these interpreters apply this prohibition to all women in all congregations for all time, effectively ripping the verse out of its context and treating it as a proof text.

Earlier in this chapter a significant amount of evidence was presented to counter these conclusions. The context here is the need for order in the assembly (14:27, 31, 33a, 40). The silence required of certain disruptive wives had to do with the point of their disruption, as it did with the tongue speakers and prophets earlier in chapter 14. The tongue speakers and prophets were not being completely silenced but only as respects the point of their disruption of the order in the assembly. Why should it be any different for these wives? The inconsistency of doing so is obvious.

There are, however, other features of the context that are equally relevant to this discussion. If we take Paul at his word in his description of this Corinthian assembly, women *did* speak in it. One of the ways Paul's discussion in I Corinthians 14 reflects this is in the manner in which he addresses the church. His normal term for addressing the church is the plural "brethren" (*adelphoi*), which in the context of all 69 of his uses of the word to address churches refers to the *whole* church, both men and women. Note that in 14:26 and 39 he addresses his references to speaking roles in the assembly to "brethren," that is, "brothers and sisters."

An even stronger indication that Paul includes women among the speakers in the assembly is the repeated use of the plural personal pronoun, "you" (*humeis*, eleven times), and the plural adjective, "all" (*pantes*, nine times), with reference to the congregation. Twice (14:5, 18) he even combines the two words into "all of you," indicating that he is addressing the entire congregation. Yet the way this chapter is read by many is to take most of the uses of "all" to mean "half" (men only). For example, "I want all of you [that is, men only] to speak in tongues" (14:5). In fact, in 14:31, where Paul uses "all" three times, by that interpretation "all" would mean "half" one time and "all" (men and women) twice—in the same sentence! Further, in 14:23 "the *whole* church" (*hē ekklēsia holē*) and "all" (*pantes*) refer to the same individuals as speaking in tongues. But according to this line of interpretation, flowing from the belief that 14:34 prohibits every woman from addressing the assembly in any formal way, "all" in this verse would mean "half" of the church, not the "whole" church.

Does it not seem strange that Paul would repeatedly express himself by such an inclusive word as "all" if he means "let the women be silent in the assemblies" to be absolute? Many writers talk about an apparent conflict between 11:5 and 14:34. What about this inconsistency? Perhaps the problem is not with Paul but with the modern reader. What if Paul actually meant "all" to mean "all" earlier in the chapter? How might that call into question the common proof text interpretation of 14:34 that forbids all women in every congregation for all time from speaking in the assembly in any way?

Conclusions

THE TRADITIONAL INTERPRETATION OF I COR. 14:34-35 has been that Paul is forbidding all women in the congregation from speaking in any formal way in the regular assemblies. This study calls that interpretation into serious question. Such a reading of 14:34a, "let the women be silent in the assemblies," as an absolute prohibition for all Christian women is the result of wresting this verse from its context and treating it in proof text fashion. The passage in context, however, presents the careful reader with several clear points.

First, far from preventing any formal speech to the church, Paul only addresses some repeated disruptive questioning of other speakers. His solution is to silence that kind of speaking in the same way he did the disruptive practices of tongue speakers and prophets. In all three cases the required silence refers only to the point of disruption, not to all other vocal participation in the assembly. In fact, by Paul's repeated reference to "all" of the congregation or "the *whole* congregation" (14:23) as exercising various speaking gifts in the assembly, he is affirming that both men and women were thus engaged.

Second, the women in the passage are a limited group of wives who had Christian husbands in the assembly on a given day who were capable of enabling their wives' learning by answering their questions at home. No other women are addressed in this passage, so this is not a blanket prohibition of all women speaking in any way in these assemblies.

Third, Paul supports his prohibition in two ways. The first, an appeal to "the law" (14:34) turns out to be so general and ambiguous that no interpreter has been able to do any more than make an educated guess as to his meaning. It, therefore, is of little or no help in arriving at Paul's overall meaning in the passage. The other reason was local custom ("shameful," 14:35). Here Paul is reminding these Christian wives how they should conduct themselves around other people in the presence of their husbands. They should not be acting in a way that is regarded as shameful.

Finally, nothing in I Corinthians 14 suggests a modification of the picture of women in the assemblies presented in I Corinthians 11. Along with the men and with no distinction between them, save their head covering, women spoke in the assembly by praying and prophesying. In fact, as Paul repeatedly affirms in I Corinthians 14, "all," both men and women, were engaged in various types of speaking in the assemblies. How tragic it is that I Cor. 14:34-35 has been used by so many for so long to silence all women in every assembly in every place for all time!

Discussion Questions

1. What evidence is there in 14:34-35 and its context to help us determine the type of speech by these women Paul wants to stop?

2. The passage singles out married women in the congregation who had Christian husbands present in the assembly on a given day who could answer their questions at home. What are the other possible categories of women in the assembly Paul does not address?

3. What is the evidence that women did, in fact, speak in the Corinthian assemblies?

4. How do you resolve the supposed conflict between I Cor. 11:5 and 14:34?

CHAPTER ELEVEN

I Timothy 2:8-15

While I Cor. 14:34-35 has played a pivotal role in discussions about what women may do in the assembly, I Tim. 2:8-15 has been more central to prohibiting women from praying out loud in the assembly, and 2:12 specifically has been used to place women in general under men in general not only in the assembly but in all other areas of church life. It is fitting, then, that our study should conclude with I Tim. 2:8-15.

Exposition

Prayer

I desire that the men pray in every place, lifting up holy hands without anger and arguing. Likewise women to adorn themselves in appropriate attire with modesty and moderation, not with braided hair and gold or pearls or expensive clothing, but what is fitting for women professing piety, namely, through good works. (2:8-10)

Men Praying (2:8). Paul begins this paragraph on congregational prayer in 2:1, goes into an aside in 2:5 and returns to prayer in 2:8. It is clear that by his use of the word *anēr* ("man") in 2:8 and *gunē* ("woman") in 2:9-10 Paul is giving different instructions to the men and women of the congregation. In fact, the concern about anger (*orgē*) and arguing or verbal conflict (*dialogismos*) is more appropriate to men than to women. This is an understandable corrective, given Paul's charge to Timothy to put a stop to the unhealthy speech of his opponents.

Women Praying (or not) (2:9-10). The literature on these two verses centers on (1) whether women are *included* in the discussion of prayer in the assembly, (2) whether they are *excluded*, and (3) if excluded, whether that exclusion extends to other settings as well. We will examine these three matters in order.

Included. The evidence usually presented that Paul ends his discussion of congregation prayer in 2:8, rather than 2:10, is twofold: (1) the reference to prayer is not specifically repeated in 2:9 and (2) while the infinitive of "pray" (*proseuchomai*) completes the main verb in 2:8, where men are under discussion, a different infinitive, "adorn" (*kosmeō*), completes the main verb in 2:9. The evidence in support of the view that Paul still has prayer under consideration in 2:9-10 is also twofold: (1) the "likewise" (*hōsautōs*) at the beginning of 2:9 connects what these women were doing with what the men were doing and (2) prayer has been the overall topic under discussion since 2:1, so if it were not in 2:9-10, then these verses would represent a change in subject with no apparent reason in the context. Thus, Paul's sense would be "likewise, I desire women, *when they pray*, to adorn themselves. . . ." The Greek text allows either meaning.

Excluded. It is one thing to conclude that Paul does not *include* women in his discussion of prayer in this passage

and quite another to infer that he intends to *exclude* women
from those who may pray in the assembly. There is a serious
flaw in this line of reasoning. If "I desire that the men pray"
(2:8) means that women may not do so in the assembly, it
should follow that "I desire that women adorn themselves
in appropriate attire with modesty and moderation" (2:9)
means that men may not do that in the assembly. Yet, who
would argue that?

Let's look at a similar example in the Pastoral Epistles. In
Tit. 2:2-8 Paul describes the character and behavior required
of older men, older women, and younger men. As in I Tim.
2:9, the three are connected by the word "likewise." Is it reasonable to conclude that because a trait of one is mentioned
the others may not exhibit that characteristic? For instance,
older men are to be "sound in faith, love and perseverance"
(2:2). Does this prevent older women and younger men from
doing the same? Or older women are to be "teachers of what
is good" (2:3). Does that preclude the other two from being
that kind of teacher? Surely the fact that Paul includes men in
the praying does not mean that women are excluded from it.

Other Settings? The words "in every place" (*en panti topō*) in
2:8 provide the key to determining the setting Paul has in
mind for these instructions. According to extensive research
by Everett Ferguson (1991), in Jewish and early Christian
sources, many of them under the influence of Mal. 1:11,
"place" (*topos*) had become a technical term for a place of
worship. Thus, "in every place" in I Tim. 2:8 refers to every
place where the church meets to worship. Just as was true in
I Corinthians 11 and 14, Paul is here talking about what goes
on in the regular Christian assemblies. Failure to recognize
this specialized meaning of "in every place" here has led to
much speculation about the circumstances in which women

are not allowed to pray, including in the presence of men, in chain prayers in devotionals, and in public. Paul put none of these restrictions in the text. He is referring to prayer in the assembly, period.

The conclusion is inescapable. Nothing Paul wrote in 2:8-10 in any way restricts women's freedom to pray out loud in the assembly or any other setting. Such restrictions add elements to the text that are simply not there. Further, suggesting that this passage forbids women to pray out loud in the assembly would make the practice in Ephesus inconsistent with that in Corinth, where women did pray out loud in that setting (I Cor. 11:5). If we are using NT practice as our guide, limiting women's freedom to pray in our assemblies today is a grave departure from apostolic practice and needs to end.

Teaching

Let a woman/wife learn in quietness in all submissiveness. I do not permit a woman/wife to teach or to have authority over/domineer a man/husband, but to be in quietness. (2:11-12)

THE OVERALL POINT PAUL IS DISCUSSING IN THESE VERSES has to do with women teaching. However, three elements in the context need attention before examining that: (1) the identity of the "woman" (*gunē*), (2) the meaning of "silence" (*hēsuchia*), and (3) the requirement for "submissiveness" (*hupotagē*). For the larger question of teaching (*didaskō*), did Paul's point about these women teaching have to do with the fact *that* they were teaching, *what* they were teaching, and/or *how* they were teaching? We will consider the three contextual elements first.

Three Contextual Elements

*Identity of the "Woman" (*gunē*).* That Paul uses the word *gunē* in these two verses with the meaning "wife" rather than "woman" is seen in his triple use of the creation narrative immediately in 2:13-15. As has been pointed out repeatedly in this book, everything in Genesis 1-3 is about the relationship of a particular man and woman with each other. The woman was formed for a particular man, her husband (2:13). The woman sinned when she was deceived by the serpent in the presence of her husband (2:14). Among the consequences of the woman's sin was increased pain in childbirth (2:15), a result of an intimate activity between a particular man and woman. This all suggests that Paul's restrictions on teaching only apply to some wives, not to all the women of the congregation.

*Quiteness (*hēsuchia*).* Paul employs the word translated "silence" or "quietness" (*hēsuchia*) only here and in II Th. 3:12, where it means the opposite of being disorderly. While in certain contexts the word group to which *hēsuchia* belongs may refer to vocal silence, it has more to do with such conditions as quietness, lack of disturbance, tranquility, or good order (Bauer, 2000, p. 440). This is well illustrated in Luke's use of *hēsuchia* in Acts 22:2, its only other occurrence in the NT. The setting is the mob violence against Paul when he had been suspected of taking a Greek into the Temple (21:28-36). Luke describes the contrast when Paul motioned with his hands and the people greatly quieted down (*sigē*, 21:40), getting even quieter (*hēsuchia*, 22:2) when they heard him speaking in their native tongue. From this example it is evident that although there can be a definite verbal element to the quietness expressed by *hēsuchia*, the contrast with the absolute pandemonium in the crowd before Paul spoke shows that it is much more than that.

This fits perfectly with what we find in I Tim. 2:11-12. Just as with the men who were told to behave themselves in the assembly (without anger and arguing, 2:8), whatever these women were doing was disruptive to the tranquility or quietness (*hēsuchia*) that should characterize Christian meetings. Thus, *hēsuchia* in 2:11-12 refers to much more than speaking. It indicates quiet, well-ordered behavior, just as its cognate adjective (*hēsuchios*, "quiet") does earlier in the chapter (2:2).

*Submissiveness (*hupotagē*).* The word translated "submissiveness" in 2:11 (*hupotagē*) is used only four times in NT, all of them by Paul. Only in this current usage does it relate to women, but the cognate verb, *hupotassō*, ("to submit") does five times in Paul. Four of these occurrences refer to married women's voluntary submission to their husbands, and the fifth to a wife without specifying to whom she is to submit. So here in I Timothy 2, where there are already other indications that Paul is discussing wives and not women in general, it is reasonable to take this as another indication that Paul is referring specifically to married women. The reference to these wives' submissiveness while learning raises an additional question. To whom was their submissiveness to be addressed? As in the similar case in I Cor. 14:34, Paul does not tell us. Perhaps it is best simply to say that these wives were to exhibit a submissive demeanor while learning and leave it at that.

One final matter about the use of the word "submissiveness" here is its relationship with the word translated "have authority" (*authenteō*) in 2:12. In connection with the structure of 2:11-12, "in quietness" (*en hēsuchia*) frames 2:11-12, "learn" (*manthanō*, 2:11) balances out "teach" (*didaskō*, 2:12), and "submissiveness" balances out "have authority."

The precise relationship between the two will be discussed in the treatment of *authenteō* below.

Paul's Point about These Women's Teaching

That *They Were Teaching*. Note that Paul is here correcting something that has already been going on. He does not simply pull this out of the air. What this means is that these wives were teaching in the assemblies in Ephesus. Think about the significance of that. This is the most Pauline of all churches, a congregation whose leadership would have been intimately familiar with any restrictions Paul placed on women's activities during the assembly. Further, Timothy, one of Paul's closest evangelistic companions, was in Ephesus when he received this letter (1:3). If Paul's universal practice was to prevent women from teaching during the assembly, why would the leaders and Timothy, knowing this, have been allowing it? The answer is obvious. It was not the *fact* that these wives were teaching during the assembly but something else. Something about either the *content* of what they were teaching and/or the *manner* in which they were doing it was troubling Paul.

What *They Were Teaching*. It is well known that opposition to false teaching is prominent in I Timothy. After a short salutation, Paul immediately launches into a charge to Timothy to confront false teachers (1:3). Numerous interpreters have inferred from this and the reference to "the woman's" deception in 2:14 that the women in 2:12 had likewise been deceived by false teachers and were therefore forbidden to teach their false message. However, direct evidence of this is lacking, though it is certainly possible. Perhaps it is best here to grant that Paul's reason for these women to stop teaching in the assemblies in Ephesus *may* have been his problem with *what* they were teaching. However, we will be on much firmer ground in examining the evidence that he was primarily concerned with *how* they were teaching. For that we need to consider the way Paul uses the Greek word, *authenteō* ("exercise authority" or "domineer") in 2:12.

How *They Were Teaching*. The ability to arrive at a definitive conclusion on Paul's use of the Greek word for "exercise authority"/"domineer" (*authenteō*) in 2:12 is complicated by the fact that (1) its only use in the entire Greek Bible is here, (2) there are very few known examples of the word's being employed prior to Paul's own use in 2:12, and (3) interpreters generally define the word to fit conclusions they have already reached on women speaking in Christian assemblies. Nevertheless, we have not been left completely in the dark here. The most comprehensive study of Paul's use of *authenteō* here by a member of the Churches of Christ was done by Carroll Osburn (1982). Osburn sifts through all the confusing studies on this word and argues rather convincingly that "domineer" best suits Paul's point in this passage. He shows that *authenteō* explains the *manner* in which these women were teaching. Thus, he sees Paul's point as not permitting a woman to teach (a) man in a domineering way.

This meshes well with the fact that in the original Paul uses "in quietness" at the beginning and end of 2:11-12. By framing his whole statement by this phrase, he shows that maintaining tranquility in the assembly is his main concern, not unlike what we found in Paul's concern for order in the Corinthian assemblies (I Cor. 14:27, 31, 33, 40). When others were teaching and these women were learning, they were not exhibiting proper submissiveness (*hupotagē*). When they were teaching they were exhibiting an aggressiveness or assertiveness (*authenteō*) either over the men present or their own husbands that upset the tranquility of the assembly. Thus, Paul is not forbidding women to teach in the assembly but is concerned with the *manner* in which they were teaching.

One more matter relating to the word *authenteō* requires attention before moving to 2:13-15. In much of the literature on women in the church it has become axiomatic that women may not lead men in any activity in the church, either in or out of the assembly. No passage in the NT teaches that, but some have inferred as much from the phrase, "*authenteō* man," in 2:12. Thus, based solely on this questionable interpretation of 2:12, many have limited the right of all our women to be in any leadership role where men are involved. The interpretation is questionable, first because, as Ferguson pointed out (1991, pp. 65-73; 2003, p. 34), the phrase "in every place" in 2:8 indicates that Paul is limiting his teaching in this passage to what happens in the assembly. Second, *authenteō* does not even mean "to lead." Though this word is difficult to define, by any definition it is a stronger word than that. Note further that, according to Jesus, in the kingdom the exercise of authority has no place in leading (Matt. 20:25-28=Mark 10:42-45). Thus, Paul is not talking about leading in 2:12, but something much more negative than that. If men had been the ones guilty of whatever *authenteō* involves, rather than certain wives, surely Paul would have stopped them as well.

Allusions to the Creation Narrative

For Adam was formed first, then Eve. And Adam was not deceived, but the woman, having been deceived, became a transgressor. But she will be saved through childbearing, if they remain in faith and love and holiness with self-control. (2:13-15)

IN THE ONGOING DISPUTE OVER WOMEN IN THE CHURCH, these three verses, especially the first two, have played a key role. For those who support traditional limitations on women in the church, 2:11-12 states *what* they should and should not do, and 2:13-15 offers the *why*. Certainly the introductory word, "for" (*gar*), shows that Paul connects the two, but unfortunately he does not state what that connection is. He merely makes these allusions to Genesis 2-3 without specifying *how* they support his instructions for women/wives during the teaching-learning activities in the assembly. All this was dealt with in chapter five of this book. Although points made there will be summarized here, the reader is encouraged to reread that discussion.

Adam Formed First, Then Eve (2:13). This verse makes a verbal allusion to Gen. 2:7-8, 15 (*plassō*, "*to form*") and a non-verbal allusion to the fashioning of Eve from a part of Adam in Gen. 2:21-22. The earlier discussion in chapter five makes the following key points: (1) the context in Genesis 2 has to do with the companionship of the first married couple; (2) this indicates that Paul has in mind offenses, like Eve, of *married* women; and (3) those offenses have to do with the way a wife should act in the presence of or toward her husband.

Adam Not Deceived but the Woman Was (2:14). This verse is a verbal allusion to Gen. 3:13, where the woman made the excuse that the serpent had *deceived* (*exapataō*) her. Just as with 2:13, Paul does not tell us what his point is in verse 14. Until recently the rather uniform understanding of his meaning has been that Paul is arguing that woman's ability to resist temptation is weaker than man's; therefore she should not be allowed to teach or be in a position of authority over men (2:12). Few now would make that argument, for reasons noted in chapter five of this book. To those reasons can be added the fact that Paul directs older women to teach younger women (Tit. 2:3-5) and speaks favorably of women who taught the Scriptures to a child (II Tim. 1:5, 3:15). Is it reasonable to conclude that women may teach women and children, who are more vulnerable to deception, but not men, who are less so?

We are left, then, to find an alternative to the traditional interpretation of 2:14, one that takes seriously the particular situation in Ephesus Paul's words are meant to address. As discussed above, Paul is responding either to the content or the manner of these women's teaching, more likely the latter. So, rather than the potential of deception being Paul's concern, he would instead be using the woman in Genesis 3 as an analogy or cautionary biblical illustration to support his restriction on these wives' teaching, much like the way he did in II Cor. 11:3. "Trouble in Paradise" came when, through deception, the woman became a transgressor (Gen. 3:6, 13; I Tim. 2:14). This is analogous to the lack of submissiveness in the behavior in the assembly in Ephesus that was detrimental to the tranquility of those meetings (2:11-12).

Nevertheless, it is assumed among those who hold to the traditional limitations on women in the church that the way Paul uses the Genesis creation narrative in 2:13-14 shows that his instructions in 2:11-12 are timeless and universal, going back to God's original intent for women. Therefore, rather than being a response to a particular situation in Ephesus, they apply to every woman in every congregation for all time. There are two major flaws in this line of reasoning.

First, Paul uses the creation narrative in I Cor. 11:8-9 to support his point that "the wife is the glory of the husband" (11:7). That point in turn supports his instruction about women covering their heads when they pray and prophesy. Yet, many of the same interpreters who argue that Paul's use of Genesis 2-3 in I Tim. 2:13-14 prohibits women from teaching for all time deny that his instructions about women's head covering need to be followed today. You can't have it both ways.

Second, if Paul's use of the creation narrative in 2:13-14 is proof that the prohibition of women teaching and having authority over men is a universal and timeless precept, why does it show up so late in the Bible? It should have been true throughout the OT. Yet, in the OT women did these things with God's approval and at times at His direction.

Saved through Childbearing (2:15). This verse presents the modern reader with questions whose answers have eluded its interpreters. We do not know who the subject of the verb "saved" is, the precise meaning of that verb in this context, or who the subject of the verb "continue" is. However, what to us is a strange statement must have been clear to Timothy, because it is the capstone of Paul's whole argument. The most that can be said with confidence is that the verse appears to be an allusion to Gen. 3:16a, "she will bear children." Here once again, just as in 2:13-14, this points to *married* women, not women in general.

Conclusions

INTERPRETERS HAVE USED I TIMOTHY 2 TO LIMIT WOMen's Christian service more than any other text in the entire Bible. Among many who would staunchly defend Paul against the charge of contradicting himself are those who oddly maintain that women may not pray out loud in the assembly, in contradiction to the clear teaching of I Cor. 11:5. Arguing that denying women the right to teach men is based on God's universal will going all the way back to the creation, these expositors lack an explanation of how their theory contradicts the God-approved and often God-prompted teaching of men by women in the OT. And by a deft redefinition of the word "authority" to mean "leading" of any kind, women have had their ability to serve tragically abridged, despite Jesus' instructions about how his disciples are to lead and serve. In this chapter, the evidence for these conclusions has been examined and found wanting.

Clearly I Timothy 2 is a complex passage, rendered all the more so by our lack of understanding of certain key features of the background. However, gaps in our knowledge do not account for all the confusion that has been generated around this passage. Some of it is attributable to flawed interpretive methods. The time has come for serious Bible students to take another look as this crucial passage dealing with women in the church.

Discussion Questions

1. Did the women pray in the assemblies in Ephesus just as the men did? Explain why you think so.

2. What is the rationale for concluding that women were already teaching in the assemblies in this church where Paul had spent so much time? Do you agree with it?

3. Does Paul teach that women are more susceptible to temptation than men? Explain your answer.

4. What is the evidence to support or reject the traditional conclusion that Paul's appeal to the Genesis creation narrative in 2:13-14 indicates that he intended his words about women in 2:11-12 to apply to all women in every congregation for all time?

CHAPTER TWELVE

The End of the Matter

This book has been an attempt to shed light on the biblical passages relevant to the question of women in the church by using the tools of exegesis to answer the first two questions about the text: what does it say? and what did it mean? In the process, certain reconstructions of other interpreters have frequently been challenged by noting when they have imported into the text elements that are not there. Given the fact that the multitude of questions we want to ask of the text far exceeds the available evidence, we often must make educated guesses. Where we get into trouble is when we do not recognize the impact assumptions we bring to a passage have on our conclusions about the meaning of the text or when the guesses we make in reconstructing the situation in a passage become "evidence" to support other conclusions. These shortcomings occur far too often in writings on this topic.

Because I have tried as much as possible to limit this inquiry to the exegetical study of the first two questions, to this point the third question—what *does* it mean?—has often lingered in the background. Since I have spent hundreds of hours over much of a lifetime investigating these passages, my readers would be perfectly justified in asking what my "educated guess" is about the situation addressed in them. After all, exegesis is not complete if it does not try to synthesize elements that have been analyzed to death. This synthesis cannot answer the third question, but it can try to make sense of the situation of the original speakers, writers, and readers so those insights can guide us as we attempt to apply God's eternal word to our vastly different time and place. So here goes my best guess.

Proposed Situation for Women in the Church and Home in the First Century

CHRISTIANITY WAS BORN INTO A WORLD IN WHICH THE normal spheres and expectations of men and women were very different. In Jesus' world in the East things were more restrictive for women, but as we move into Paul's world in the West, we find growing freedom, even in public, during the Hellenistic period. This varied from place to place, but what did not vary was the norm that married women had a special role in the home and a particular obligation to their husbands. This mixture of diversity in the application of the growing freedom of women and uniformity about their role as wives and "managers of their household" (I Tim. 5:14) is the setting in which NT speakers and writers found themselves.

Enter Jesus of Nazareth. Under the influence of the Pharisees (rabbis), first-century Palestine was very conservative and traditional in its mores and customs on the position and conduct of women both in the home and in public. Yet time after time Jesus demonstrated that he did not see himself bound by these conventions, even to the point of openly flaunting them. From this it is clear that Jesus was ushering in a new way of looking at and interacting with women. Clearly a new wind was blowing, and it was coming directly from the author of Christianity.

In spite of a few verses in Paul's writings that sound strange to the modern ear, on balance we find in the NT, following Jesus' example, an enormous leap forward for the status of Christian women. However, due to the natural aversion to anything new in the Jewish, Greek and Roman settings, the first Christians had to be careful about their reputation with both local governments and the populace. They picked their battles for the sake of the mission. Paul alludes to this concern frequently in his writings. Not surprisingly, it surfaces in his discussions about women, especially wives, in the church, his teaching about head coverings in I Corinthians 11 being a prime example.

Many have suggested a parallel between the way Paul treats women and slaves. While "there is neither Jew nor Greek. . . slave nor free. . .male and female" (Gal. 3:28), the full working out of the Christian application of those relationships in the church has been an ongoing task. The difficult matter of race relations in the church in the West in the last two or three centuries is an embarrassing example. There are hints in the NT (e.g., Philemon 8, 16) about what ultimately happened in the attitude toward slavery in the West in more modern times, but Christians during the first few generations were in no position to challenge slavery.

In a similar way, it is my educated opinion that the often-hostile situation in which the early Christians found themselves and/or their concern for outsiders' receptivity to the gospel are the reasons they at times needed to avoid upsetting local norms about women's, especially wives,' behavior. Thus, in those passages in I Corinthians and I Timothy that seem to go against the flow of the significant elevation of women by Jesus and in the rest of the NT, we need to ask whether there was something in the specific situation in Corinth or Ephesus that can account for it. When we do this, those passages that seem so out of sync with the rest of the NT become much more understandable as Paul's instructions for specific situations on the ground in Corinth and Ephesus, rather than as directives for every congregation in every place for all time.

Two Largely Neglected Topics

IN MOST OF THE WRITING ON THIS TOPIC THAT HAS BEEN done in the Churches of Christ, two matters have not received the attention they deserve. The first is the extent to which the relationship between Christian husbands and wives is in play in the key Pauline passages in I Corinthians and I Timothy. The other is that most early Christian assemblies were in a house-church setting and the impact that has on the understanding of these passages.

Husbands and Wives versus Men and Women

THE ENORMOUS CONFUSION THAT HAS BEEN GENERATED around this issue goes back to the unwarranted application of the Genesis creation narrative to men and women in general in the church, rather than to husbands and wives. In fact, there is no clear passage in the entire Bible that places women in subordination to men in any other relationship than at home. Further, in all the subordination passages in the NT where it is clear whether men and women or husbands and wives are in view, the latter is always the case. So why is it that some interpreters, going against the flow, see I Cor. 11:3 as referring to women and men in general in the church, rather than to wives and husbands, as in all the unambiguous passages? Or why do many writers apply the statement about women being silent in the churches to women in general, when the passage clearly identifies certain *wives* as those to whom Paul is referring (I Cor. 14:34-35)? Or why do so many interpreters understand the women being discussed in I Tim. 2:11-15 as all women, when the context from the two references to the Genesis creation narrative (2:13-14) and the mention of childbearing (2:15) make it clear that Paul is talking about *married* women?

After much reflection on these and other questions, it is my considered opinion that in all three of the key Pauline texts (I Cor. 11, 14, and I Tim. 2) Paul is dealing with an affront by certain wives to the way, in their social setting, they should conduct themselves as married women. Additionally, some of the key details of those passages, rather than referring to God's intent for all wives for every situation for all time, reflect instead their unique setting. They are Paul's application of God's will for husbands and wives to a specific situation.

Assemblies in House Churches

WE TWENTY-FIRST CENTURY CHRISTIANS PROBABLY FIND it difficult to place ourselves in the shoes of our early brothers and sisters who had no church buildings. Especially as a new congregation was formed, its normal place of assembly was in a home. When the congregation was of sufficient size and it was able to meet in the more expansive Roman home of one of the well-to-do members, the line between private and public could become blurred. This might cause a particular problem for members of the household where the church was meeting. Should the women in the home dress and adorn themselves as they normally would at home or should it resemble more their public attire, since so many guests would be present and it technically was not a family event? This may sound trivial to us, but it may very well be in the background of Paul's concern with attire and adornment in the assemblies in I Corinthians 11 and I Timothy 2.

A description of my own involvement as a member of two house churches illustrates how different that setting is from what most of us experience every week. In both congregations, we were a small group meeting in someone's living room. In one we were fewer than ten and in the other just under twenty. In that kind of intimate setting, would it have made sense to enforce a hard and fast rule that during the Bible lesson a woman could not quietly ask a question or make a comment? If no man was capable of leading a song, would God have been upset with us if a capable woman started the songs and helped us get through them? Should we have forbidden a woman from getting up out of her chair to pass the communion elements to someone sitting on a nearby couch? I can tell you that in both of those congregations we talked and interacted as people normally do in a living room, and no one thought any of the women were out of line.

Would it have been any different in a house church in the first century? So much of what has been written about what women may or may not do in our assemblies reflects the perspective of our formal, public worship services. How different might our conclusions be if we simply considered the fact that so often they were meeting in homes.

A Word to Church Leaders

Safe Course?

I HAVE OCCASIONALLY HEARD THE ARGUMENT MADE THAT when we are not sure of a course of action we should err on the side of the safe option. In practice, however, this principle is often difficult to apply, because it is not always easy to identify which course is the safe one. The issue of women in the church is one of those cases. It is argued, for example, that if we are not certain that a woman may do this or that in the assembly, the *safe* course would be for her not to do it. But is this the safe course? What if we state it a different way? If we are not certain that a woman may *not* do this or that in the assembly, how is it the safe course before God to abridge her freedom in Christ by not allowing her to do it? There is no safe course here. Either choice has the potential of being against God's will. In fact, limiting the freedom of action of half of our adult fellow Christians is anything but a safe course. We need only to look at Galatians 5 to understand the seriousness of limiting another Christian's freedom in Christ. As a church leader, I do not want to have to answer for wrongly abridging anyone's freedom, male or female, when I stand before my Creator.

Why Now?

WE ARE INCREASINGLY BECOMING OUT OF STEP WITH OUR world. We are, of course, called to be separate, to be holy. The problem comes when we have no firm biblical basis for being different. The early church was trying to establish itself in a world that was suspicious of them, if not openly hostile. It had to address the impact of being culturally offensive on both their safety and the reputation of the gospel message. It is vital that we too not unnecessarily stand apart from our culture in ways that limit receptivity to the gospel. Assuming for the moment that we may have limited women's participation in affairs of the church in ways that cannot be justified by Scripture, here is why it matters and why the clock is ticking.

- The church is the only place in our Western society where women are limited. What does that say to the non-Christian or even to our own women and teenage girls?

- Our young people have already moved on, both in their views on this matter, and for many of them as soon as they have the freedom to do so, from our fellowship.

- While we should be leading our culture in doing the right thing, we have sometimes needed to be steered by our world. The issues of the use of the Bible to justify slavery in the American South in the nineteenth century and race relations in the church in the twentieth century are distressing examples. Sometimes it has taken our world to wake us up to reconsider what we believe the Bible teaches. In my lifetime, the treatment of African American brothers and sisters in many congregations and some of our Christian colleges shows that we were behind our culture in this matter of right and wrong. It took the momentum of our culture to wake us up to restudy our Bibles, repent of our sinful behavior, and change.

I know how difficult tackling such a tough question as women in the church is for congregational leaders. It has the potential of being divisive. If our Bible study should lead to a change in practice in any way, people may leave and sister congregations will view us suspiciously at best. The topic is complex enough that a serious examination would probably take a great deal of time and energy from other vital congregational priorities. The list could go on and on. I know, because I have lived through it. For many years our congregation studied the matter in dribs and drabs, but that did not satisfy the thirst the majority of our members had for searching for the truth on this matter, regardless of where our quest led us. Finally, our elders decided that this was one area where we could not afford to get it wrong, so after doing their own Bible study, they led the congregation in a comprehensive study of its own. Because our goal was to achieve congregational consensus, respecting everyone's conscience, the process was neither short nor easy. In the end we followed through on our commitment to change our practice only where our understanding of the Bible led us. Because we had not cut corners, as we altered our practice, the elders and congregation were able to move forward together.

I am not presenting what our leaders did as a model for others. What I am saying is that the matter of how we have treated our women is one that will not go away. It will only intensify. At some point we will all have to face it head on. Given our Restoration commitment to patterning our practice on the Bible, what we ultimately do must be based on disciplined Bible study, not simply a rehashing of traditional interpretations and superficial study. Yes, the clock is ticking. Our world has moved on. Our young people are walking out the door. How much longer can we put off settling this once and for all?

Concluding Remarks

SADLY, I COR. 14:34 AND I TIM. 2:12 HAVE BEEN A PLAY-ground for biblical expositors. These verses have been isolated from their contexts and treated in proof text fashion to support some bizarre applications in our modern-day church. Women have been silenced in our assemblies to the point that speaking alone they dare not utter a word heard by men. In many places, not only have their voices never been heard in prayer in the assembly, but any time Christians get together, even for small social gatherings, only men are called on to pray. In some homes, husbands never experience the spiritual pleasure of hearing their wives or baptized teenage daughters pray. Once a boy is baptized he may no longer hear his mother's gentle prayers. In most congregations women are not allowed to pass a communion tray to more than just the person seated next to them. According to some, a woman may not sign for the deaf or interpret for someone speaking in a language unknown to the congregation. With a deft hand, many writers have transformed "*authenteō* a man" in I Tim. 2:12 into "*lead* a man" and applied it to all sorts of situations, preventing women from leading any congregational ministry that includes men as participants.

All of these and many other unwarranted and harmful attempts to silence our women and limit their service to the Master seem to stem from two unbiblical sources. The first is the belief that the Genesis creation narrative places women in general under men in general and that that applies to the church as well. As has been observed multiple times in this book, such a view is without biblical foundation. The other is the rejection of Jesus' view of leadership and authority as it applies to his disciples and the reversion to that of "the rulers of the Gentiles." Thus, for a woman humbly and quietly to lead a prayer in the assembly (in the same manner, by the way, that men usually pray) is somehow regarded as an act of authority over the men present. How Jesus must weep at our human interpretations and disregard of his words!

Discussion Questions

1. Do you believe that differences among Christians about what women may do in the assembly and the broader ministry of the church are significant enough to divide us?

2. Describe any experience you may have had in a more informal Sunday worship service, such as at a retreat, in a house church, or in a hotel room while traveling. Relate that experience to the traditional interpretation of I Cor. 14:34 that prevents women from speaking up at all in church.

3. Can you think of any examples of where the church may have been unduly influenced by our culture? What about examples of where the culture may have pushed us in the right direction?

4. If you were a leader of your congregation, what factors would you weigh in making the difficult decision about changing a long-standing congregational practice based on fresh study of the Scriptures?

Bibliography

Bauer, Walter, William F. Arndt, F. Wilbur Gingrich, and Frederick W. Danker. *A Greek-English Lexicon of the New Testament and Other Early Christian Literature*. Third edition. Chicago: The University of Chicago Press, 2000.

Daley, M. O. *God's Woman*, "Introduction." In *God's Woman*. Clifton, TX: Nichol Publishing Company, 1938.

Dudrey, Russ. "'Submit Yourselves to One Another': A Socio-Historical Look at the Household Code of Ephesians 5:15-6:9." *Restoration Quarterly* 41:1 (1999): 27-44.

Evans, Mary. *Woman in the Bible*. Carlisle, Cumbria: Paternoster Press, 1983.

Ferguson, Everett. "Of Veils and Virgins: Greek, Roman, Jewish, and Early Christian Practices." *Restoration Quarterly* 56:4 (2014): 223-43.

—. "Τόπος in 1 Timothy 2:8." *Restoration Quarterly* 33:2 (1991): 65-73.

—. *Women in the Church*. Chickasha, OK: Yeoman Press, 2003.

Grasham, William W. *Truth for Today Commentary: Genesis 1-22*. Searcy, AR: Resource Publications, 2014.

Hardeman, N. B. "News and Notes." *Gospel Advocate* 80 (Oct. 20, 1938): 992.

Lemmons, Reuel. "C. R. Nichol Passes Away at Clifton." *Firm Foundation* (July 18, 1961): 450.

Lightfoot, Neil R. *The Role of Women: New Testament Perspectives*. Memphis, TN: Student Association Press, 1978.

Montefiore, C. G. *Rabbinic Literature and Gospel Teachings*. New York: KTAV Publishing House, 1970.

Nichol. C. R. *God's Woman*. Clifton, TX: Nichol Publishing Company, 1938.

Osburn, Carroll. "ΑΥΘΕΝΤΕΩ (1 Timothy 2:12)." *Restoration Quarterly* 25:1 (1982): 1-12.

—. *Women in the Church: Reclaiming the Ideal*. Abilene, TX: ACU Press, 2001.

Oster, Jr., Richard E. "When Men Wore Veils to Worship: The Historical Context of 1 Corinthians 11.4." *New Testament Studies* 34 (1988): 481-505.

Patterson, Nobel. "C. R. Nichol." *2004 Freed-Hardeman University Lectures*. Henderson, TN: Freed-Hardeman University, 2004: 341-45.

Made in the USA
Columbia, SC
23 August 2021

43424999R00093